HE RODE WITH DEATH AT HIS BACK

Half the men in the county had formed posses to hunt Hugh Kingmead down. They had him surrounded; he was like a rabbit caught in a trap. They were just waiting to close in and kill him.

Kingmead had been in this kind of trap once before. He'd managed to escape, to run away, once before. But his running days were over. This time he was going to stay and fight for his rights—and his life....

Books by Ernest Haycox

Alder Gulch
Action By Night
Chaffee of Roaring Horse
Free Grass
Head of The Mountain
On The Prod
Return of A Fighter
A Rider of The High Mesa
Riders West
The Silver Desert
Starlight Rider
Sundown Jim
The Wild Bunch
Whispering Range

Published by
WARNER PAPERBACK LIBRARY

**ARE THERE WARNER PAPERBACKS
YOU WANT BUT CANNOT FIND IN YOUR LOCAL STORES?**

You can get any Warner Paperback Library title in print. Simply send title and retail price, plus 25¢ to cover mailing and handling costs for each book desired, to:

WARNER PAPERBACK LIBRARY
P.O. BOX 690
NEW YORK, N.Y. 10019

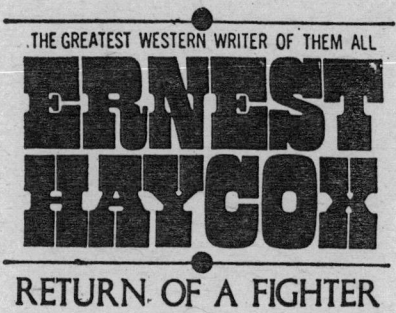

RETURN OF A FIGHTER

WARNER PAPERBACK LIBRARY

A Warner Communications Company

WARNER PAPERBACK LIBRARY EDITION
First Printing: September, 1971
Second Printing: November, 1972
Third Printing: June, 1975

Copyright 1929, by Short Stories Inc.
Copyright renewed 1956, by Jill Marie Haycox
All rights reserved.

Cover illustration by Jim Sharpe

Warner Paperback Library is a division of Warner Books, Inc.,
75 Rockefeller Plaza, New York, N.Y. 10019.

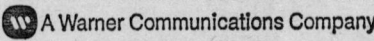 A Warner Communications Company

Printed in the United States of America

Not associated with Warner Press, Inc. of Anderson, Indiana

CONTENTS

Chapter One: Sagebrush Bound 7
Chapter Two: A Troubled Country 15
Chapter Three: Bad News At The Double Arrow 33
Chapter Four: Murder Trail 41
Chapter Five: Gesher Strikes 57
Chapter Six: The Mob At Night 75
Chapter Seven: The Chase 97
Chapter Eight: The Fight On The Bench 105
Chapter Nine: The Struggle For Sun Ford 127

Chapter One

SAGEBRUSH BOUND

"WHAT OUTFIT, GENTS?" Hugh Kingmead leaned across the observation car rail, reading the brands on the cattle through the slats of the car on the siding at Ogallala. Strange brands, yet a part of the life he had once known, harbingers of the land into which he now headed again.

The punchers who squatted by the caboose of the cattle train looked up. A tourist they would have disregarded, or no more than passively acknowledged. But they recognized Hugh Kingmead. He was of their class and not even eight years in the East could conceal the signals on his lean, sharp face. From the square-toed shoes, the suit hanging loosely to his spare frame, to the cropped black cowlick falling over his forehead, he was plainly marked. They heard the slight slur of his words and they saw the lazy way he carried himself. So one of them answered, "Three Y—Green River."

"Good year?"

"Oh, fair enough. Kinda poor calf drop, though. How's Eastern fleshpots?"

"You boys deliver your stuff and don't tarry none about coming back."

The puncher was cheerfully and cynically disbelieving. "Yuh must've stayed too long yoreself. Can allus tell a singed duck by the way it quacks. Slim an' me aim to do our paintin' judicious. Ample but judicious. Yuh headin' west?"

"Back to the old pasture," drawled Hugh.

"Back to beans an' gravel, yuh mean," said the puncher. "Yuh'd ought to have more sense. Some men is hogs for punishment."

The puncher didn't mean that. He was only grousing. He grinned at Hugh; Hugh grinned back. The Limited's air brakes sighed, the line of cars moved slowly. "So long, good luck," called Hugh. "Don't buck the other man's game."

The puncher flung up an arm, his homely, grinning face warped in the hot sun. "I'm sensible. A hundred percent is all I want for my money. So long."

Hugh Kingmead relaxed in his chair on the observation platform and looked across the rail at the sand and sage and the familiar windmills skimming against the horizon. His own history came back to him in fragments, in scenes, in hopes and omens and achievements. Eight years was a long time to live alone in a big city; a man, if he wished, could have the solitude of a miner up in the Western hills. And he had wished it so, excepting only the business contacts made in his quarters just off Wall Street. Eight years —from nineteen to twenty-seven. Behind that was a chapter he had deliberately closed, and he had thought closed for good, till a doctor had opened it once more.

The city was not for him, the doctor had said. If the Creator had been pleased to give him rain to wash his face and sun to soak his skin, why should he hide behind a wall called business? "Why, with the whole world to pick from and no strings to tie you," the medico had asked, "must you live here? Go back, Kingmead, go on back where you're a free agent."

So Kingmead was on his way back. He wondered what had made him break away so easily. What was the idea of leaving the sure fortune that lay just within reach after struggling eight years? And why wasn't he sorry? At the end of those years of scheming and fighting—in which he couldn't recall having laughed aloud—a trick of mind had set him aside and now he looked back as a spectator. He thought he had been rooted. Now he discovered he never had taken an ounce of nourishment out of that foreign soil. He wondered about Ruby Lusk. Ruby had licked him in one fight and he had run away from the man. Well, that's what it amounted to. Now he was going back, with a tough fight on his hands.

But already he felt more alive and the numbness had left his tissues. "By Judas," he murmured, and then again, "By Judas," and a network of wrinkles sprang about his eyes and he smiled.

Then he became aware of someone laughing directly beside him—a strangely gay and warm laugh. He turned, feeling betrayed by his own tongue; thus far on the trip he had lived in complete isolation, rubbing elbows with fellow passengers yet scarcely knowing them to be present.

It was a girl sitting in the adjoining chair, a girl of about twenty-one, dressed to the fashion and with a small hat jammed down over jet hair. It gave her an air of jauntiness, an air further heightened by the rose-petal tint of her cheeks and by eyes that looked up to him with frank amusement. She was not a small girl, rather she was robustly built, free-limbed. Hugh Kingmead found himself grinning, not exactly understanding why he should. And out of plain habit his attention dropped to her hands to find them bare of rings. The only jewelry she wore was a cameo pendant that bobbed from side to side with the turn of her trim head.

"I've wanted through seven states to hear you speak," she said. "There's a woman's curiosity at its worst. At Chicago I suspected you to be Western. Now I'm certain."

"When a fellow gets lonely for his own breed," said Hugh, "he's apt to shoot off steam. Did you get on at Chicago?"

Her smile grew. "I've sat across from you all the way from New York. No, I'm aware you didn't see me. But I suspected you to be Western—the real Western."

"This," said Hugh, growing sober and throwing his hand outward toward the undulating prairie, "is something I've missed."

"For how long?"

"Eight odd years," murmured Hugh. "Eight years out of Oregon."

"Oregon? Then I can understand. I've only been exiled twelve months, but it has seemed like a thousand. I live southeast of Bend and I'll be glad to get back."

Kingmead's attention narrowed and grew sharply intent. He looked at her with a more direct interest; something akin to recognition stirred in his mind. It seemed to him he had seen her before or that her features resembled those of a family he knew. If she lived southeast of Bend he ought to know her name—providing she had been raised in the country. He was on the point of giving his own name when an inner warning stopped him. He was going back into trouble and it wouldn't help to reveal his identity too soon. The West didn't change much from year to year. The same night wind played across the high desert and the same coyotes howled along the ridges. No, the West didn't change; the old feuds and antagonisms might be sleeping, but they would wake again at his return. Barring death, Ruby Lusk would be around Sun Ford yet. Hugh Kingmead's features settled and chilled at the memory of the man. One unsettled debt stretched across those years, concerning himself and Ruby. Squat, immense-chested Ruby

11

Lusk with the swart face of a desert savage and the murky eyes of an animal.

The girl made a small motion with her hand; for a moment she watched him, frowning a little. A porter came to the platform, murmuring, "It's ready, miss." She rose, the smile returning; it flashed on Hugh an instant and then she disappeared down the car corridor.

He saw very little of her after that, for he kept to the observation and she stayed in her own car. At Baker, Oregon, she got off and he watched her go across the station walk, erect and buoyant, carrying her bags with the freedom of a man. As the train pulled away and she caught sight of him standing on the observation platform her chin rose and she smiled. With the smile came the old Western farewell, "Be good, cowboy."

"The same to you," said Hugh Kingmead. His attention fell to the twin initials on her bags—*H.S.* Then the humor deserted his face. He knew at that moment who she was and the knowledge brought with it a quick depression. Of course she wouldn't recognize him; she had only seen him twice or so and eight years ago she was but a gangling girl in pigtails, riding the range on a spotted pony. Helena Starrett.

She'll be taking the stage across country, thought Hugh. *Down the John Day and through Mitchell. Next time she sees me she'll know—and then there won't be any smile.*

He left the train the following morning at the Dalles and took a feeder south to Bend. Late in the afternoon he walked through the streets that once had been familiar and now were changed. Bend had grown some—its streets ran farther into the sagebrush, its stores made a greater showing. It had lost some of its frontier atmosphere; there weren't so many horses hitched to the racks. The depression grew as he had the feeling that this was going to be a sorry homecoming. Was he to be an alien in his own land?

It was time to eat and rest, but he couldn't sleep in town with the desert calling him out. Directly after supper he went to a stable on the edge of town and dickered for a horse. The proprietor, judging Hugh by his clothes, walked several animals around the corrals and went through the customary patter about teeth and hock action. Hugh only grinned, pointing his finger to an animal off at a corner. The proprietor looked more observantly at Hugh.

"Hell, I thought you was a stranger! Say, ain't I seen you before?"

"Let it ride," said Hugh. The stable owner didn't recognize him, though he remembered the stable owner. "You got a saddle around here with a Nelson tree?"

He bought his rig, went to a hardware store and got a box of forty-four shells for his gun. That gun was the sole relic of the old days; he had carried it with him to the East—a scarred, long-barreled weapon better than forty years old. His father had carried it before him and in dying had passed it on. Later, after he had bought range clothes and changed into them at the stable, he dropped the gun into its holster with the distinct feeling that the act forever put the East behind. He grinned and rode away into the desert. Some miles out he made a dry camp beneath a juniper tree and stared upward at the stars, hearing the old song of the night breeze and the old chant of the coyotes. Out of the vast solitude of the high desert came the ancient voices, bidding him welcome.

"Well," he murmured to himself, "no matter what happens or how short a time I live, I'm home."

At dusk the next evening Hugh Kingmead rode into Sun Ford, returning to a fight he had abandoned eight years ago.

Sun Ford, this summer's night, was unchanged. The same dusty streets ran along between the same dusty, battered buildings. The same kerosene lamps winked out of the same windows. And in front of the largest structure in the sleepy cattle town he stopped to read a sign that had been there since Sun Ford was a Government post: *Loren A. Gesher—Gen'l Mchdse—Bank—Lands—Breeding Stock.*

"Loren," said Hugh Kingmead softly to himself, "you're going to be surprised. Unpleasantly. I reckon you've got a still tighter grip on the district than ever. All right. I'm better fixed to fight you now. But where's your hired gunman, Mister Ruby Lusk?"

He wasn't ready yet to have the town know of his return and so he scouted the restaurant before going in. It was empty and he ate a solitary meal. The saloon doors, across the street, were open and as he left the restaurant he saw a group loitering at a card table. He got on his horse and rode on out, noting here and there the blurred bulk of men in the shadows or on the hotel porch. Eastward he turned with a quickening anticipation. A few miles over there was the ranch that once had been his and now was Loren A. Gesher's. The elder Kingmead had borrowed from Gesher and that obligation Hugh had inherited. Then Gesher had seen to it that Kingmead stock—Sawhorse brand—was rustled and poisoned from the ranges. Ruby Lusk had a hand in that.

"Ruby will pay me for it," said Hugh Kingmead, passing out of the town.

No sooner had he cleared the street than a man moved from the hotel porch toward the saloon—moved with the haste of one bearing important news. Midway in his journey he met a younger chap and halted.

"Say," he demanded, "did you see what I seen?"

"Nope," said the younger one. "I ain't been drinkin' lately. What was it?"

"Oh, by the cross-eyed Maggie! Hugh Kingmead's back!"

Chapter Two

A TROUBLED COUNTRY

"Who's Kingmead?" demanded the younger one.

"Why—Oh, that's right. You hain't been in the country more'n a year. Well, Hugh Kingmead's the man who can agitate this country from muzzle to tail. Jupiter, but it's good news! Good news for ev'body but Hugh Kingmead. I got to spread this."

"What about him?" insisted the younger one. But the other was already ten yards off and moving at a dog-trot. "I got to spread this," he flung back over his shoulder.

The younger man turned and made for the sanctum of the *Sun Ford Roundup*. He was a somewhat disillusioned fellow by the name of Harold Quiggett who, having saved a little money from a city reporter's job, had come to rangeland and bought a weekly, thus fulfilling the desire every good newspaperman owns. But there is a tremendous gap between city reporting and country reporting and in a year Harold Quiggett had burned his fingers many times and learned many things. He went directly to the back files of the *Roundup* and began riffling through them.

"Kingmead—Kingmead. Seems I've heard the name. Great Scott, what a terrible make-up they used on this sheet. I'd like to change it, but every mossback in the country would shout. Kingmead, um. Wonder if I could find some innocent to buy me out? What's the use of owning a paper when a gossip like Tade Borth spreads news faster than I get it? Kingmead—ahuh." He found the item he wanted, dated more than eight years previously, and skimmed down the column:

Justice goes on the rocks again. What's the matter with public opinion in this county? The second jury to try Hugh Kingmead for the murder of Colonel Ansel Starrett reported disagreement today. Prosecuting Attorney Best says he won't try the case again. Kingmead goes free and a beloved and sturdy pioneer's death goes unavenged. What's the matter with public opinion?

Quiggett groaned. "There's a sample of everything wrong in reporting. And still they eat it up. Evidently the law of libel doesn't apply hereabouts. So justice went on the rocks. Might add it's been on the rocks ever since I hit this sinkhole. There ain't no justice unless it's Loren Gesher's kind. Bet this former owner was a Gesher man down to the dandruff."

The next item to attract his attention briefly chronicled the disappearance of Hugh Kingmead from the country, after which followed another tirade on the abortion of justice. Quiggett replaced the files and returned to the street, struggling with his professional instinct. He thought, *Here's a good story. A story that will interest everybody. And I don't dare use it. Can't turn around in this county without stepping on somebody's toes. No, I've got to sit on the fence and write editorials about civic improvement or the degeneration of the adjoining towns. Hell!*

He stopped at the saloon and looked through the doorway toward a table that had been occupied all afternoon by three particular players. The sight only increased his disgust and he moved toward the hotel porch. "At said table," he muttered, "is the weak relic of the illustrious Starrett name gambling off his inheritance." His observant eyes also noted Sun Ford's leading gossip, old Tade Borth, emerging from Loren Gesher's store like a cat that had licked up a pan of cream.

For almost a year that poker table had seen the same three men assembled around it. At certain hours and on certain days it seemed to be reserved to them alone, nor was a fourth man ever welcome in the game. At nights many spectators gathered around, for this was a blood game and not a casual pastime of friends. Not only that but each man bore a certain questionable importance in the county and there was drama in the way they each held their cards and bet their chips. Chiloquin Charley almost never spoke; Ruby Lusk maintained a heavy, close-lidded joviality; Elmo Starrett's fitful and bickering temper rose and fell in the manner of a smoldering forge fire. On the table always stood a bottle and a litter of cigarettes. Around it lay torn cards—ripped apart by Elmo Starrett's impatient fists. Every ten deals brought a new deck. In the beginning this strange game had been for moderate stakes. Now, with Elmo Starrett playing against his own money and his fortune badly dissipated, it was a plunging and vicious brand of poker. Starrett long since had thrown caution to the winds and bet his hands, good or bad, with a headlong abandon.

Elmo was a gambler at heart. Upon his youthful and not very broad shoulders had fallen the management of the Starrett ranch after the death of Colonel Ansel Starrett. An administrator's control during Elmo's juvenile years had kept him from squandering his part of the estate. Later,

Helena Starrett had checked her brother's slack tastes. But upon her departure for the East Elmo played and lost. And in losing became the more surly and unmanageable. There was nothing attractive about the boy. He was skinny and peaked of features—one of those types which can be made handsome only by the print of a rugged and honest character. No such character could be seen on Elmo's slack lips or in his hazel eyes; plainly he was somewhat beyond that border where the good and the bad elements contest for a man and the issue is determined. Elmo's habitual expression was one of anger or one of cynical pouting.

He lost a bet on an ill-judged bluff and in losing surrendered the last chip in his pile. Lusk raked in the pot with a chubby fist and his copper-colored face twisted into a grin. "Bad luck allus comes direct after supper, kid. Here's another stack of chips. Let's go. Evenin's young yet."

Elmo shook his bleached yellow head and poured himself a drink. It went down in one toss and seemed to touch off his temper. He stared across the table at Lusk. "What the hell you so anxious to play for? Ain't you won enough for one night?"

"Don't be that way, kid," said Lusk, rolling a cigarette. His narrow eyes rolled around the circle of bystanders and fell. "You ain't able to say I don't give yuh a chance to win back."

Chiloquin Charley rested, a passive figure in the chair, never saying a word. He seemed to be brooding over a dark problem. Chiloquin Charley was a straight, lean, and bronzed man who rode the ranges, yet never in any outfit's pay and never with company. Once he had laughed easily. That had been in the days when Hugh Kingmead ran the Sawhorse brand. He seldom had smiled since.

Elmo grumbled and tipped back his chair. "I should've been in Baker day before yesterday. Sis wanted me to meet her. Damn this game, anyhow. I could've still met her at

Mitchell last night. Expect she's home by now. Listen, Ruby, I'm through. I'm goin' home. You've took the last chip from me. The very last one, hear that?"

Ruby's dark face was momentarily obscured by cigarette smoke. He sat like a rock in the chair, shoulders spilling over the sides of it. This man's history was perfectly known to Sun Ford and the surrounding country. He was hated, despised, and feared; yet no matter what others thought of him, his tremendous and ill-proportioned body inspired awe in the beholder. He was short of leg—so short that to walk a dozen yards caused him to sweat. He was, likewise, abnormally short of arm. When he stood erect his hands fell less than four inches below the hip bones, and because of that physical peculiarity his right palm always rested directly beside, and in contact with, the low-slung butt of his gun. This shortness of limb helped accentuate the remarkable bulk and depth of his chest, the muscles of which ran upward and outward to his shoulder tips and seemed to double back along his arms, making them appear like great pistons coupled to an engine. Other series of muscles stood out on a neck that once had been measured in Gesher's store at nineteen inches around. It was Ruby Lusk's boast he never had found a shirt big enough to button at the collar; there was a woman in Sun Ford who ripped and enlarged all his new shirts.

Atop this unwieldy frame perched a head that apparently had been beaten out of copper. Such was the color and texture of it save where the white scars of conflict had been gouged in the surface. His nose was flattened, his lips were thick and sank against his teeth as if they had at one time been crushed there. Down over an extraordinarily narrow forehead fell a jet and oily cowlick, and beneath this were two almond-shaped eyes that served Ruby Lusk very well to conceal his emotions when he chose. For all such emotions had to pass through a kind of muddy film, or to lie back behind that film. Men had a hard time reading motives in the eyes of this man. It was Ruby's habit, when hard pressed, to laugh and rub his ears—ears that had been at one time pierced for rings.

He laughed now and pushed the stack across to Elmo Starrett. "You'll play again, kid. You ain't through."

"What makes you think so?" snapped Elmo, sallow cheeks tingling with red. "What makes you so damn sure about that, Ruby?"

"Men don't ever quit while they're losin', kid. Here's your stack."

Elmo made an abrupt motion with his arm. Pencil and paper dropped to the table. "I'm through. How much I owe you?"

Lusk studied the youth with a closer and colder glance. "A thousand even, kid."

Elmo Starrett scrawled off an I.O.U. for the amount and threw it at Lusk. Then he turned to Chiloquin Charley. "I've squared you already out of pocket. We're quits." He took a heavy pull from the bottle and stood up, burning with a sudden heat. "I've spent enough in this joint to buy it. Mark me, Lusk. Some day I'm bringin' my riders in to riddle and burn this stink-hole down to the sills."

"All two of 'em, eh?" grinned Ruby, jibing at Starrett's depleted ranch force. He shoved the chips farther forward. "It's a young evenin', kid. Sit up an' gamble like a veteran."

Young Starrett's forehead glistened with sweat; he studied the chips with a pinched, almost avaricious interest and perhaps would have gone on with the game if Tade Borth had not chosen that moment to enter and set off the bomb that was to rock this country end to end. He slid casually up to Ruby Lusk. "Gesher wants you should come see him right off," he muttered. And raising his chin toward the crowd he drawled out the news that burned his tongue.

"You gents'll be interested to know Hugh Kingmead jes' rode in an' rode outa town again only a few minutes ago."

Ruby Lusk's fist crashed against the table; he sprang up from the chair, face squeezed to a hard and furious knot. "Yuh lie, yuh damned scandalmonger!"

A breath of wind seemed to pass through and stir the small crowd. Elmo Starrett's cheeks were dead white and he was shaking. "Which way?" he muttered. "Which way did he go?"

Chiloquin Charley, alone of the crowd, sat in his chair. He had his face downward and nobody saw the wild flash that passed over it—an expression that might have been fear or hope or despair. As all the others crowded about Tade Borth he slipped quietly from the place.

"I saw him with m' own eyes," grumbled Borth and regarded them triumphantly. "I saw him go."

"Yuh lie!" thundered Ruby Lusk. His fist touched the gossip carrier and the man swayed like a leaf under the invisible pressure. "Yuh lie! Any more stories like that an' I'll put a row o' button holes all the way through yuh!"

"Leggo me!" snarled Borth. "I saw him, I tell you! And Gesher wants yuh in a hustle."

"Why didn't yuh come to me right off then?" boomed Lusk.

"Took it to the gent who's most interested in the news," muttered Borth, squirming free.

Lusk put his head down and plowed through the bystanders, never waiting for them to move aside. Elmo Starrett took another drink and spoke to the ceiling. "I got to get home—I got to get home in a hurry." He followed Lusk through the lane of bystanders, catching the backwash of softly muttered oaths. The crowd milled toward the bar and in the crossfire of talk Harold Quiggett, just entering, heard the whole story of Hugh Kingmead and felt as well the oppressive hostility that clung to each man's speech.

Kingmead's return was the pitch that fed the slumbering flame of the old mob impulse. Men in this country never forget.

Ruby Lusk vanished inside Gesher's store. Chiloquin Charley slipped down the street to the stable and took a currycomb and brush from the rack. The stable roustabout marked this with an ironic commentary. "Yuh tended that brute o' yours once today. He got royal blood or somethin'?" Whatever else the man had a mind to say died on his tongue. Chiloquin Charley's eyes were afire in the semi-darkness of the lantern-lit place. He drew the currycomb across his pony's hide with the mechanical move of one who thought of other things—and thought of them with a gripping intensity.

Ruby Lusk came out of Loren Gesher's presently and galloped out of town with three other men at his heels, taking the direction Kingmead had earlier gone.

The old Kingmead ranch was eight miles from Sun Ford and a half mile off the main trail. Toward this Hugh Kingmead rode. At first he went leisurely, assailed by the memories of the older time when he had swept through the night with blood running high and his chosen friends traveling beside him. Life had been a very simple affair then and to ride eighty miles to a dance was no more than a youthful gesture. The groan of the saddle beneath him and the clink of bridle chains brought all this back with a peculiar sensation of loneliness and regret. The country was changed; it seemed more deserted. He passed three ranch-houses in a row standing tenantless. And he remembered that once they had been occupied by upstanding cattlemen and fine families; and he had danced in them and made love in his boyish way. Eight years and more ago.

"Travel," said he, breaking the spell. "There's the Alvords, the Lovenights, and the Langells—all gone from the country. I wonder if Loren Gesher bought 'em out or squeezed 'em out? The man always had an obsession to own this end of the county by himself. An obsession. Travel, pony."

The animal's leg muscles bunched and he fled along the trail. Hugh Kingmead stared sharply at the familiar landmarks along the dark countryside, turned out and headed toward the bench. Presently the outline of a house stopped him. He got down with the smell of lilacs in his nostrils, and all the accumulated homesickness and foreboding rose and spilled over as he recognized that sweet scent. His mother had planted it years before, and still it stood as token and remembrance of his boyhood. Hugh Kingmead stood quite still for a moment, staring up at the dim stars. This was his land and why had he ever left it?

He shook his head clear of the trailing sadness and led the pony around to a rear shed. The walls of the house even in the darkness seemed settled and loose; the rear door stood open and half off its hinges. He went through to the kitchen and struck a match. In the moment's light he saw the litter of dirt and papers on the floor. Between the cracked boards a vine crawled up. The match went out and he proceeded down a hallway to the living-room. Even before he lit another match he knew that this room had been used as some kind of rendezvous. The smell of stale tobacco and of whisky clung to the air; all sorts of rubbish were under his feet and when the match's small glow broke the darkness he saw before him the litter and relics common to a barroom. There was a table and a lamp standing upon it and scattered chips and a battered deck. Chairs, some overturned and partly broken, were lying about. Bottles and tobacco cans, castoff boots, a torn shirt, and a bunk with a blue blanket upon it—these things met his eyes. The next minute his fingers snuffed out the light and he drew back against the room wall, standing quite still. Somebody came up the trail.

"They saw me in town," he murmured. "On my heels right soon. Ruby Lusk moves fast—when Gesher gives him orders."

Three or four of them. They stopped out front and presently a voice unknown to him hailed crisply. "Hello, the house."

There was an old closet opening off the living-room. Hugh Kingmead retreated into its narrow confines and drew the door shut, hearing a guttural and impatient phrase: "He wouldn't be here anyhow."

They came across the porch and inside, heavy bodies springing the loose flooring. One of those bodies pressed against the closet door and there remained until a point of light gushed through the keyhole.

"What made you think he'd come here?"

And the answering voice seemed to light a swift and hot fire in Hugh Kingmead's chest. Lusk was speaking. "Every dawg comes back to its own hole. Look around, boys."

They went questing through the house. They climbed the stairs and poked through the upper rooms and gathered again in the living-room. "This dawg ain't in this hole. Listen, Ruby, he's too slick a sucker to come right back where he knows we'd be lookin' for him. My bet is he's out sulkin' on the bench. What's he figger to do, anyhow? It's a damn poor country for a Kingmead. He oughta know it."

"Don't you misjudge the gent none," warned Lusk. "I know him. I've played hound an' rabbit enough with him. He ain't nobody's fool. But it don't matter where he is, we got our orders to find him."

"Gesher want him jailed on that old charge again, Ruby?"

A kind of muffled and sardonic laugh reached Kingmead. "Yuh didn't ketch the drift o' my statement, Slip. I said we got orders to find him. If that ain't clear enough I will add we're supposed to leave him jus' where we find him. Dead."

"Why?"

Lusk's voice thickened. "Because Gesher's afraid o' him. Because I want his hide nailed to my door, by Judas Priest! He's too dangerous to let free. First thing you know we'll be ridin' along the trail and he'll reach us with a rifle shot. Wouldn't put it past him. If he's here, it shore means he's nursed a grudge a long time an' he's aimin' to pay off. Now listen; we're on a war footin' till we git him. I want my orders obeyed down to the dot. And no talkin'. Understand—no talkin' our business. Gesher's got a strong holt on this section but they's still a few gents who'd like to join Kingmead an' fight out the old battle. The news is all over the range right now—and spreadin'. So we got to be careful. Slip, you ride over to the south meadows and pick up the boys there. Meet me at—"

The rest of it Kingmead lost in the general movement of bodies out the door and across the porch. The light had been extinguished; a few moments later they were away down the trail. Kingmead let himself out of the closet, got his horse out of the shed, and cut across country for the bench. Up there was an old line cabin that once had served as a meeting place for him and the friends he once had known.

"The death warrant's out," he muttered. "They certainly don't give a man much time to get settled. Gesher always played a close hand. And Lusk will sure dog me like the plague. Now that I'm back, what's the next move?"

He didn't know. He had returned on an impulse to a land in which his life was worth very little. He had only one weapon—money. Inside his breast pocket lay the reapings of his eight Eastern years; he stood ready to hit at Gesher in this manner if he could. But, as he climbed upward along the bench into the deepening shadows and the profound silence, it seemed to him money was a singularly futile weapon in this country and especially against a man such as Gesher. One lesson Hugh Kingmead had learned in the East: money was nothing more than time put in a concrete form. Where time was valuable, money was valuable. Out here time meant very little. It rolled along through the hot days and the sharp, cold nights, through the weeks and the months and the years; and men accustomed themselves to its slow tempo. They thought in terms of seasons, not in terms of days. What could money do?

He arrived in front of a squat shadow surrounded by pines, and dismounted. This was the line camp. As he came nearer he saw it had suffered the same ravages of time as had the ranch-house. To sleep inside was unwise; he led the horse deep into the pines, unsaddled and picketed the animal, and made himself a cold camp. Rolled in his blanket, he stared up through the branches and saw the North Star gleaming against the velvet vault and, on the edge of sleep, he thought again of what he should do. Gesher's hand lay across the land like a sullen shadow. The man was obsessed with the idea of property and power, just as some more civilized person might have a passion for precious jewels, and he pursued his purpose like a war general. He had patience, he could wear others down by waiting; but when waiting seemed unfit for the occasion he could strike with uncanny speed. Kingmead grinned wryly at the great star. Evidently Gesher took the latter course now. The death warrant was out for Hugh Kingmead. With that thought he fell asleep.

It seemed only a moment later that he awoke, and in waking rose to an elbow. He swore softly at himself for the movement. Eight years had taken the edge from his animal instincts; he should have rested still. Over by the line cabin something moved cautiously, something tapped the cabin wall. The sound melted into the infinite silence of the night, like a raindrop falling to the ocean, and for several moments nothing broke the suspense. Kingmead's arm crawled to his gun. He unfolded his blanket and rose up, standing beside a pine and protected by the pine's opaque shadow. The intruder moved, a horse's hoof touched a rock and there came a rippling, sibilant noise of boots sliding across ground and the abrasion of corduroy breeches.

Kingmead stepped around a semicircle on his toes; he arrived at the edge of the pines and saw the dim black bulk of man and horse against the lesser blackness of the night. The man was a yard from the horse, ten yards from Hugh. One man—or an advance scout for the rest of Ruby Lusk's party? He waited, and it pleased him that the rhythm of his heart was unbroken against his chest. He was still sound, he had not lost everything. The intruder's shadow wavered. And over the soft summer air palpitated a low whistle that ran along the double-noted call of the quail. Kingmead's gun fell away from the dim target and he bent ahead as if trying to pierce the vague screen. Caution warned him; yet that signal bridged the years and made them seem but a day. He was back again to the time of the old fight, to the time he and his friends challenged like this. He drew a breath.

"Who's that?"

The man's shadow rose to a straight, thin line. "Hugh, old kid?"

"Yeah."

"It's me—Izee Beulah."

"Light a match."

There was a fumbling, an arc of orange light. It broke the shadows and over the short space Hugh Kingmead saw a face he never thought to see again. A high-bridged nose, coal black eyebrows above deep sockets, a long thin mouth seated in burned skin. It was Izee. Hugh muttered, "Blow it out, Izee," and crossed the ground at great strides. "You damned old duffer! By Judas, I'm glad to see you!"

A pair of fists sank into Hugh Kingmead's shoulders like vises. Izee muttered something that went awry and covered it up by swearing with a fervid and pungent eloquence. "I heard you'd come home," he went on. "Listen, you got a hell of a nerve walkin' into sorrow this way. Yuh oughtn't to done it, but I'm glad to see yuh! Was over at that High Camp honky-tonk when the news came through. Caused more excitement than the news o' the Spanish War. It's all over the county now. I hit for here. Knowed you'd have to hide out."

"Well, Izee, you sure sound the same to me," said Hugh, struggling with his words. "You're the first sign of old times since I got back. Izee, don't ever go away from your home range. It's a jolt comin' back to find things different, friends scattered, no place to go. I've been sort of melancholy. You sound better to me than eight banjos playin' the fandango. Remember that time all eight of us broke up the party at Big Six? Happy days!"

"Happy days."

They fell silent, the spell of old times catching their memories; and each a little ashamed of spilling over. These two were by nature silent men and only the meeting, with all it meant, could have caused them to break the barriers. Izee's arms dropped. Apropos of nothing at all he made a casual observation. "It's twelve o'clock."

"Thought you were one of Ruby's lads," said Hugh. "I was cached in the old place when he and some of the others rode in. Heard how the cards lay."

"Open season on yuh, Hugh?"

"Yeah."

"Knew it," grunted Izee. "Yo're too much dynamite to let live. Gesher's allus been a little scared of yuh. Ruby's bragged he'd mount your horns if he ever got the chance. How's tricks been, Hugh?"

"Fair. But don't ever leave home range, Izee. By Judas, it's lonesome. What you been doing?"

"Oh, travelin' around. Stayin' out of the county mostly. Workin' on the Bell A Bar now."

"What happened to the rest of the gang?"

Izee delayed the answer. He rolled a cigarette in the darkness, and by the ensuing match light Hugh Kingmead saw his old partner's face settle and grow grim. "Ain't a long story none," muttered Izee. "Pete Brock fell off a hoss right after yuh left. That's one. Whitey and Slim Loree sauntered 'way south. Never heard of 'em since. Think they're in Arizona. That's three. Dud Mead and Tammy and Rube Mitchell are workin' on the Bell A Bar with me. That's six. Bill Bixby's nursin' along some cows on his own hook." And both of them chuckled softly at the memory of this partner. "His outfit's growin'—one way and another. Bill's morals are all right but sometimes his eyesight fails him when he finds a stray cow. That's seven. Luke Lane tried to match Ruby Lusk's draw three years ago—the damn fool! An' that's eight."

Nothing is so disheartening as to rake over dead ashes, to realize that what is past is gone and can never be recalled, especially early youth and all the freedom and the reckless, heady luxury of life that goes with it. That time would never come again and thus these two men who had been so inseparable, who had fought so hard and ridden so recklessly and still were no more aged than twenty-eight, pondered somberly over the old chapter.

Hugh stirred. "You left out one, Izee."

"Yeah," replied Izee, dry-voiced. "I dunno what to say about Chiloquin Charley. Yuh know he sorter grew strange to us even before we all split up. Never figgered him, myself. He's around. A solitary rider. I ain't sayin' he stands in with Gesher or Ruby Lusk. Mebbe he don't. But he plays a lot of poker with Ruby and he acts mighty queer when I cross his trail, which ain't often. Like he wanted to talk and was afraid to. Used to be a gay cuss. Regular funeral advertisement now. That's all. What's on your mind, Hugh?"

"I came back to balance the account."

Izee's head moved in the shadows. "The trail's old now, Hugh. Rained out—"

"Listen, Izee, it's got to be cleared up. I aim to live here. Out in the open. I'm going to do it if I've got to smash Loren Gesher and all of Gesher's hired artists. I tucked my tail and ran once. I'm here to stay. From now on."

Izee's arm fell across Hugh Kingmead's shoulder. "If that's a declaration o' war, Hugh, count me in. Sounds like old times. Why, dammit, it is old times! I can get Dud and Tammy and Rube within three hours. Send a man for Bill Bixby and he'll drop the heifers and be here tomorrow. With you and me that's six."

"Drag you boys into a private fight—"

"Oh, you string-halted idiot, what's the matter with your head? Don't you know nothin' about this country any more?"

"Cool off, Izee. This is going to be worse than any jam we ever got in. Ten times worse."

"If we ain't good enough for yuh, Mister Kingmead, you shore can go plumb straight to hell!"

Hugh took a firm grip on himself. Even so there was a sting and a tension to his words. "It looked pretty dark to me up to now, Izee. Why, I don't know where we start or how we start, but we ride again. The Lord bless you."

"Or the devil take us," grunted Izee, relapsing to his usual taciturnity. "Done. Want me to get the boys now?"

"Let's sleep on it. Tomorrow's time enough. Get 'em then, while I ride into town and see Gesher."

"Rotten idea," said Izee. "Just natcherly a no-good idea. Don't you figger what's goin' to happen the minute yuh set foot in his private village?"

"Never let a man think you're afraid of him," declared Hugh. "And I'll go in the back door. Let's roll up."

Chapter Three

BAD NEWS AT THE DOUBLE ARROW

ELMO STARRETT RODE HOMEWARD, sparing neither quirt nor spur, and leaning forward in the saddle as he passed the shale slides and the outcrop of rock along the trail; around these infringing areas rested blacker shadows and in these shadows Kingmead might be waiting. Stray sounds bothered Elmo Starrett and vague currents of wind tormented him all along the fifteen miles to Double Arrow S. The youth had a fair amount of courage, he was a good horseman and a decent marksman; but for eight years he had lived with almost a daily reminder of Hugh Kingmead's cold-blooded and brutal murder of his father. The event had happened when Elmo was at the most impressionable age and it had left a scar. The older he grew the more sinister the figure of Kingmead became; and so he was glad to see the lights of the Double Arrow S ranch-house around the bend of the trail, even though those lights meant that his sister had returned and would demand an accounting of his neglect.

There was a genuine affection between Elmo and Helena Starrett, an affection that twined through even the most bitter of their quarrels. Thus when Elmo entered and Helena saw him, she ran across the room, crying out a welcome. Elmo whirled her around quickly, lifted her off her feet. "Glad to see you, Helena! By gosh, I am!"

"I'll bet!" She kissed him soundly and knocked off his hat. For a little while they rough-housed about the room, Helena asking no quarter. She had grown up, she was fair in any man's eye and she had a dignity and a carriage in any company. Still she could be a tomboy on occasion, as she was now. Elmo tried to pursue her around a table and fell completely across a chair she had thrown in front of him. He was ready to quit then and said so. Helena dropped down on the divan and for the first time got a clear and complete look at her brother. This brief tussle had left him short of breath, he was untidy, and his face and eyes revealed an unpleasant gauntness. Helena's smile slowly faded. She knew the weakness of Elmo better than he himself knew it. The youth saw trouble in the wind and rose to roll a cigarette. The trembling of his fingers only added to the giveaway.

"Why didn't you meet me at Baker, Elmo?" asked Helena.

"Oh—sort of got tied up with business," muttered Elmo.

"What business?"

"Usual run of stuff. This and that. Have a good time at the polishin'-up school, kid?"

This was a feeble and futile attempt to change the current of talk. Helena inherited all of her father's blunt directness. "Where's all the boys?"

"Billy an' Red went over to Big Six to a dance."

"Well—where's the rest of them?"

Elmo looked at the ceiling. "Fact is, Sis, I let 'em go. Save expenses."

"Wha-at!"

"Oh, shucks, don't get excited. I never wrote you about it, but we had a mighty poor winter. Lot of stuff died.

Skinny calf season this spring. Beef way down in price. Didn't need eight boys any more."

"What difference does that make?" she demanded. "Two hands—that's ridiculous on a ranch the size of Double Arrow S. You know it. We're too well established to let one poor year pinch us. We're free and unencumbered. Let's go over the ledger, Elmo. I'm curious to know where we stand. My, but you don't realize how I've missed this old place. Never again do I go East. Move the lamp over here, Mister Starrett, and go get the ledger."

"What's the hurry?" grunted Elmo, shifting uncomfortably. "Let it go to morning. I'm tired."

Helena straightened on the divan and her voice held a deceptive softness. "Been drinking some, Mister Starrett?"

"I'm free, white, and of age, ain't I?"

"Been playing poker some, Mister Starrett?"

"Cut that out! Well—a man's got to have a little fun. You've had your whirl."

"Been losing?" went on Helena, digging in like a prosecuting attorney.

"Oh—a little."

"How much?"

"None of your business!" snapped Elmo. His lips twitched and his nerves seemed under poor control. "It's my debt and I'll pay it!"

Helena got up, cheeks flushed. "Not with Double Arrow S money, Mister Starrett. If you've been papering Sun Ford with I.O.U.'s, they won't be redeemed out of our home cash box. Don't forget this ranch is half and half."

"Yeah?" snorted Elmo, quite angry. "Well, don't you forget I can do what I damn well please with my half!"

"Elmo! Is it that bad? Who to? Oh, of course it had to be—Ruby Lusk! You fool kid, didn't you know he'd make a sucker out of you? Don't you know *anything?* Elmo, buck up."

Elmo walked away from her, never saying a word. Helena dug her fists into the divan; worry creased her white forehead. Her lips tightened. "I'm sorry I left. Wouldn't have gone either if Mother hadn't made me promise away back. But that renegade horse thief can't rob us. I'm going to look over the ledger, Elmo. And if you've slopped over on my share, I'll duck right into Sun Ford and tie up every cent in the bank. We're paying no poker debts."

"Listen, Sis, don't call Lusk a horse thief. He's all right."

"If," shot back Helena, hitching up one shoulder, a signal of battle with this girl. "If I didn't call him that it would be something worse. Don't you be a ninny."

"You won't do no promiscuous ridin' around this country, either," muttered Elmo, suddenly worried. "Ain't safe."

"Why not?"

"Hugh Kingmead's back in the country."

As with others, so with Helena Starrett. The name struck her like a blow. It damped the fire in her eyes and left her in the attitude of a frightened, uncertain little girl. It was only natural that this was her reaction; Hugh Kingmead stood for the death of her father and, indirectly, for the death a little later of her mother. So he had wiped out one generation of Starretts, he had wrecked a home. And afterward, when he had gone away, the legend of evil grew about his name, connecting it with every unexplainable mystery. The county gave him the character of an utterly cold and conscienceless killer, even though it knew the Kingmead name to be a good one. Hugh Kingmead, it was explained, was the throwback in an otherwise decent line. Why else should he have killed Ansel Starrett without apparent cause—killed him from the rear and dragged the body half a mile off the road at a rope's end?

"Elmo—"

The drum and sweep of horsemen came through the door. Elmo Starrett swung about, fingers tapping the butt of his gun. Ruby Lusk's bludgeoning voice announced the party and before either of the pair could reach the door, in swept Lusk and four of his men. The man was grinning. His swift glance fell on Helena and he crossed the floor with a heavy gallantry. "Back home for good, young lady? I bet. Elmo, yuh got a sister pretty enough to turn anybody's head." And he threw back his chin and laughed at his own speech. "Yeah, shore pretty. Helena, I watched yuh crawl acrost this floor when yuh wasn't no taller'n the grass in a meadow. Said then I was goin' to wait for yuh to grow up and marry me."

"How much patience you have, Mr. Lusk," said Helena. One lash dropped toward her brother.

Ruby saw the wink. He also understood the meaning of it. But, above all other things, he had perfect faith in himself. What couldn't be accomplished one way might be done another. That was Lusk's whole philosophy, and it had worked very well for him.

He grinned broadly at the girl. His hand rose and chucked her under the chin. "Don't you fool poor old Ruby—"

The girl stepped aside; her white hand streaked across the space and struck Lusk's black visage with the echo of a gunshot.

"You ox!" she cried. "Keep your manners in the barroom, where they belong."

Ruby's flattened lips came together and for a moment the grin left him. "Huh, you ain't had no decent trainin', I can shore see. Ain't I good enough to associate with, kid?"

"You weren't good enough to associate with my father," retorted Helena. "And you knew enough to keep away from him. That goes for me. What's the idea of riding in here at this time of the night?"

Elmo intervened. "Cut that—both of you. Ruby, hang on to your paws. When you talk to sis, remember she's got a name. And it ain't 'kid.' Get it? Sis, you better hit the hay."

Ruby saluted with a bland, imperceptibly ironic gesture. Elmo was not shrewd enough to see the irony in it, but Helena saw, and understood. "What's on your chest?" she wanted to know. "This is a private house, Mr. Lusk, not a saloon."

"If I stepped on your feelin's," said Ruby with a passable grace, "I'll back up and gee over. Shore, I'm sorry. I just dropped in to pass the time with Elmo. Figgered mebbe we might play a little poker. How about it, Elmo?"

"You come a long way just to play with my brother," said Helena, growing angry. "I want to tell you something, Ruby Lusk. This outfit is paying no poker debts, so you are just the same as playing with matches. Elmo, don't be a fool."

With that she turned and went up the stairs. On the landing she looked back to see a tight and unpleasant watchfulness on Ruby Lusk's cheeks. He stared at her too closely.

In her room, her courage sagged. She heard Ruby laughing, urging her brother on with a blending of humor and contempt perfectly designed to touch the pride of the youth. She heard chairs scrape, heard chips rattle. She fell asleep, worried, and woke up later—much later, it seemed —to hear them still playing. Somebody swore, a glass shattered against the floor.

Helena got up and braced a chair against the door. The pleasure had gone out of her homecoming. This house was no longer a secure haven; it was being grimed by the presence of such a man as Lusk. And, remembering what her brother had told of affairs, she felt that something threatened her. That there was a crisis at hand. And Hugh Kingmead was back. . . .

Chapter Four

MURDER TRAIL

A LITTLE BEYOND SUNRISE the next morning Hugh Kingmead saddled and mounted for the trip into Sun Ford. From the elevation of the line cabin he swept the valley below, identifying all the old landmarks; and it came back to him now how completely his life had been formed by the peaks and ridges and draws that lay before him, flushed with the first rose light of day. The shallow river winding through the valley flashed brightly; cattle spotted the far slope. A spurt of dust rose off the Sun Ford trail, marking an early traveler. Juniper and pine and sage—and the crisp dew-touched air—all this he had owned and then had forsaken. It seemed quite impossible now, looking upon the peaceful scene, that he once had ridden with death close behind, that men lay behind ledges and tried for his life, and that half of the county had turned out in posses that chased him and formed a giant ring around him twenty miles wide. So it had been; so it would come to be again. He rolled a cigarette and started off.

"It's just natcherly a no-account idea," insisted Izee. "I don't like it."

Hugh stopped. "I don't want those buzzards thinking I'm scared of 'em, Izee. I'm going to face Gesher in his own office and have words. And I want the county to know I haven't got a guilty conscience. Maybe that'll draw a few over to my side. Anyhow, I can't just hide out and wait for things to happen. Why not go down and set the ball rolling? Somebody's got to start the parade."

"If they's a parade," predicted Izee, "it's apt to be with you in the middle as Exhibit A. Well, if you got to go, lemme ride too."

"That's out. You and the rest of the boys will be the joker I've got up my sleeve."

"Better go get 'em and bring 'em here, hadn't I?" insisted Izee.

"That," reflected Hugh, "would put a bug in Gesher's head. When he found out the old gang had dropped work and ridden for the tall brush he'd know what was up. No, Izee, you just run back and whisper to 'em. So they'll be prepared for trouble when it comes. No use of all the gang camping out until Lusk or Gesher starts war."

"I'm repeatin'—it's a no-good idea," muttered Izee. "Well, I'll hit for the ranch and do said whisperin'. Also I'll have one of the gang ride over and tell Bill Bixby. I'll keep an ear to the ground and see what the general gossip is. Be back with some grub about the same time you get here. If yuh ain't on deck by dark—"

"Don't worry," reassured Hugh, and rode down the bench.

A quarter mile off he turned to see Izee streaking southward at a dead gallop. Hugh grinned and changed his own course somewhat. He was in no particular hurry to reach Sun Ford and he wanted to identify the cattle ranging on the valley's far slope. So he zigzagged along the depressions, studying the land and reading stray sign just for the joy of warping himself back into the old habits. He arrived at the trail, idly noted the fresh hoofprints in the dust—all pointing toward Sun Ford—and crossed the small valley floor. The river was low, its turbid waters rippling on the sand bars. He forded and rode up the slope.

How can a man pick up the trail of a murder eight years old? he mused. *There's nothing left now, except maybe that somebody's conscience bothers him. And except that the county remembers it had a high old time chasing me down and trying me. They'll do it again. Folks don't change. But, by Judas Priest, there's my job. It's going to be tough.*

He stopped a few yards from a grazing steer and fastened an interested glance upon the brute's right hip. Highest up was an iron-etched Double Arrow S, the Starrett brand. Directly below this and much smaller in size was another Double Arrow S, which signified to Hugh and to the world at large that the steer had been sold. And below this vent was a third brand, LAG. That was Gesher's. The man had a half dozen other brands, bought outright from retiring ranchers or established by Gesher himself for different ranges. Hugh Kingmead reflected grimly, *The more brands, the easier to change, the easier to blotch. Gesher's slick at that. And since when has the man taken to buying stuff? Must be getting afraid of stealing it like he did once. Which is not the main point, either. How does it come a Starrett sells to Gesher? Old Ansel never had any love for the man and it sure seems like his son and daughter wouldn't change in that regard. Interesting, you bet.*

He poked around the hillside, climbed the ridge, and dropped into another miniature valley. All the stuff he saw on this particular range bore the same history on their flanks. *Starretts must be getting poor to sell wholesale like that.*

The sun marched up the sky and Hugh turned townward. The country never changed. Gesher still ruled, Gesher still extended his holdings, still stretched forth his acquisitive

44

hand. For every cow he bought he stole ten. That was what Ruby Lusk earned his money for. Hugh's eyes contracted and he studied the trail below with a hard and wary glance. This was going to be a tough fight. Then, hearing a sound, he swung in the saddle to find a girl riding up through a clump of pines toward him.

He faced about and waited. She swayed in the saddle like a veteran, she reined the pony around the rock mounds with a sure hand. And though she was dressed like a man and though an old felt hat was slouched down over her cheeks, he knew who she was. The knowledge hardened him the more; he had dreaded this meeting and now it was upon him.

She circled and drew up on his right side, raising a hand. Her head bobbed a greeting and the sunlight flashed against her eyes. "Hello, there. Say, are you riding this stuff?"

Hugh took off his hat. "I'm pleased to meet you again, Miss Starrett."

The girl looked at him more sharply. A smile broke across her lips. "Well! The Westerner on the train. Why didn't you tell me this was your country? Now wait—how did you know my name?"

"It's a name everybody in the region knows, Miss," replied Hugh, relaxing a little.

"I guess it's a good enough name," said she with a stout pride. "Let's get this straight. How does it happen you're riding my stock all plastered over with Gesher's brand? It's news to me we ever sold him any beef. When did it happen?"

"Don't know," answered Hugh, admiring the picture she made. He had seen her in woman's clothing and he knew how feminine and gay she could be. She had abandoned all that for the time; her face was puckered and businesslike. It reminded Hugh a little of old man Starrett in a fighting mood. "I'm just sight-seein', gettin' acquainted with the country once more. I guess it's news to me, likewise, that a Starrett would ever sell to Loren Gesher."

"How do you know all that?" was her blunt question.

"Fiddlesticks, have I got to *ask* your name, cowboy?"

Hugh Kingmead squared himself in the saddle, unsmiling and almost harsh. "I reckon I'd give it to you, Miss. But if you'll look right close you might know me."

She knew, even before he had finished. The fresh color drained from her cheeks. There was a withdrawing of all friendliness, a swift and startled recoiling of muscles—exactly as if she had stepped too close to a snake. Kingmead, matching her glance, saw her eyes turn to a jet blue and noted how her nostrils pinched in. For a space of thirty seconds fear and anger fought for control of the girl; she was still as death. Then she twitched a hand and the pony crowded nearer. Her chin came up and she measured him with a look that comes to a human being once and rarely more often in a normal life's period—the desire to kill. There was no mistaking the suppressed fury that constricted her face and made it like so much marble.

"Hugh—Kingmead!"

"The same."

The fury came out of her in passionate phrases. "Oh, you murderer! You yellow, rotten cur! You ran off—you coward! Now you're sneaking back, skulking around the hills to shoot somebody else in the back. You ought to be dead. You will be dead if the county finds out you're here." She stopped for want of breath. Her horse sprang away at the touch of her spurs and she reined him back. Her arm dropped to a revolver holstered on the saddle; it came up and the peace of the bright morning was shattered by the flat echo of a bullet. Kingmead never stirred.

"Take a better aim next time, Miss," said he, very quietly.

But the gun wavered and sagged in her hand. The impulse for revenge that had been stored in her so long passed, leaving her badly shaken.

She stared at him with a haunted, half-frightened look. "I might have killed you; you deserve to be killed, Hugh Kingmead."

"It may be so," said he. "But not for the reason you have in mind."

"Then what did you run away for?"

"Because I couldn't fight any longer, Miss. Did you ever hear any reason why I should have killed your father?"

"You quarreled with him over fences. Your hat was found near his body."

"I had words with him about fences," admitted Hugh Kingmead. "And so did most of the other cattlemen. Your dad had some strong ideas. As for the hat—did it ever occur to you that if I had done that shooting I would hardly have been careless enough to've left my hat in plain sight as evidence?"

She shook her head, unconvinced. "You ran away, left your ranch standing. You were afraid to stay in the country."

"You bet," was Kingmead's laconic answer. "I tucked my tail in and ran like a licked pup. A man can dodge bullets only about so long. As for the ranch, I'd lost it anyway. I was bein' rustled poor, starved out. I reckon you were too young to know anything at all about county politics at the time, Miss. You ought to know now."

She waved that away. "It's all past now. You bought yourself free. Everybody knew you bought a man on each of those juries. Well, what makes you come back to stir up all that bitterness?"

"As for buying anybody—" he began. But he changed the subject. "I'm not arguin'. I can't blame you for believin' things you hear. I reckon it's human. The reason I came back, Miss, was to find the man who did kill your father.

I came back to this county to clear up some crooked politics you ought to know about but probably don't."

"I don't believe it—not any of it," murmured Helena Starrett. "I never want to see your face—never again. Please stay away from our range."

He nodded gravely, a fine and soldierly figure in the saddle, a mature, slightly grim figure of a man whom solitude and struggle had never ceased to mold since boyhood. And there was something gallant in the way he inclined his head to her and turned away. "We believe what is easiest to believe—always. I want you to know I looked forward to meeting you as the hardest thing I had to do. It had to be done, but I would rather have taken a licking. And I guess I've taken a good many. As to stayin' away from Double Arrow S, your wishes shall be respected."

He swung down the slope. The girl watched him go. And although every fiber in her had been trained to detest the name he bore, she was yet too much of a woman to miss seeing the wistfulness on his face as he swung off. There was something about Kingmead to attract, in spite of the reputation he bore. It had attracted her on the train; and as she retraced the trail homeward, tired and dispirited and puzzled, she fought the impulse to believe his story.

He lied. Every word was a lie. All the country knew he did that. A hundred men can't be wrong. As she reassured herself, a perverse thought came to her. Not every man in the country had indicted Hugh Kingmead. There had been some loyal followers. *But they're no better than he was. Why didn't he knock the gun out of my hand?* And much later she asked herself two still more discouraging questions. *How does it come Gesher's got his brand on our stock? And where did Elmo go this morning before I got up?*

Hugh Kingmead hurried on down the slope. A mile to the east he saw a party galloping townward. Later, as he topped a commanding bald butte, he discovered still another group on the trail, approaching the faint outline that was Sun Ford. Kingmead veered and placed the butte between himself and the trail. There was far too much travel on that trail for such a summer's midmorning. It augured trouble. Galloping from one summit to another, he debated the wisdom of entering town. He had a proposition for Loren Gesher, but he knew well enough what the man's answer would be. Why go?

Well, it was a matter of pride. He wanted the county to know he wasn't afraid, that he wasn't skulking like a coyote in the hills. Thus, in a frame of mind that was both grim and reckless, he circled Sun Ford at a discreet distance and rode into the street from the north end. He saw instantly that the saloon hitching-rack was crowded with ponies. Still farther along, men loitered by the stable and the hotel. Kingmead halted in front of Gesher's store, threw over the reins and climbed the steps. He hoped that for the moment he was not observed but he could not be sure of it.

Gesher's store was a dim and lofty place with piles and sacks and boxes of mixed merchandise heaped up on the floor. Counters ran along three sides. At the rear end a door stood ajar, opening into a small office, and through it Hugh Kingmead saw a skinny and shriveled man seated in a leather padded desk chair. A single woman customer stood by one counter, talking to a clerk. Kingmead eyed this clerk closely. The man knew him very well, but the semidarkness and the clerk's nearsightedness prevented his recognition. Kingmead strolled back quietly and came to the door. Gesher's back was to him. He stepped inside, closing the door as he entered, and when Gesher looked up and around Hugh Kingmead smiled at him with a tight cheerfulness.

"How are you, Loren?" he asked.

Hugh had always admired Gesher for an unshakable, nerveless calm. The man was never caught off balance, never showed surprise. Nor did he so much as change expression now. He tilted his small head upward and stared through his steel-rimmed glasses with a cold, dead glance. Every feature was pinched and parsimonious. He was as dry as the baked clay street outside and his cheeks were marked with an incredible number of fine lines. He had never been known to drink, he didn't smoke, and he seldom raised his voice above a rasping monotone. He looked the part of an avaricious banker or of a hypocritical church elder—and indeed he was both. He looked like anything at all save what he actually was—a man who would pronounce a death judgment to gain his own ends. By-and-by he inclined his head and spoke.

"Heard you were back in town, Kingmead. Take a chair."

Hugh moved across to a corner of the room, in a position to command the door.

"No, thanks, Loren. Only came to pay my respects, knowin' you'd feel hurt if I didn't."

"We'll dispense with pleasantries, my boy," said Gesher in the same unaccented monotone. "You did an ill-judged thing in returning. The county will never permit you to stay."

"You banking on that pretty strongly, Loren?" drawled Hugh.

"Absolutely. What did you come for?"

Kingmead rolled a cigarette before replying. "Came to find out if you wanted to sell back the Sawhorse range to me."

Gesher appraised him again. "You couldn't afford it, financially or physically. Outside of that, I never sell land. I only buy."

"Or steal," suggested Kingmead.

Gesher raised a hand with a motion that seemed to say it made utterly no difference how land was acquired. "You are still rash with your statements, my boy. You won't last long."

"Not if Lusk is able to carry out your orders," replied Kingmead, grinning. He waited for Gesher's answer; none came. The man was silently admitting the fact. Kingmead grew sober. "Well, Loren, I want you to know I'm back for good. I'll be here until one of two things happens. Either you get me or I pull your house down over your ears. I ran away once. This time it's a finish fight. That's what I came to tell you."

Gesher swung his chair around to the desk, abruptly showing his back to Kingmead. "Good day," said he, and began to read.

"Tut-tut, Loren," murmured Kingmead. "You're too successful a fighter to underestimate a man. Don't underestimate me."

Gesher's chilly eyes lifted momentarily. "You are already taken care of, Kingmead. You should have learned a lesson from eight years ago. I see you have not. That's your mistake. I never underestimate, nor overestimate. Good day."

There was an absolute finality about the words, quite as if Loren Gesher had already marked Hugh Kingmead from the list of opponents. Hugh shrugged his broad shoulders and let himself out of the office and into the dark store with the strange feeling that he had overheard his obituary. One thing he realized: Gesher had grown tremendously more powerful and self-confident in the intervening eight years. That was revealed in the man's carriage; it was further revealed as Hugh stepped upon the store porch. The street, busy with people when he had slipped into town, was quiet now. A solitary figure stood opposite the store, leaning against a building wall and watching Kingmead's pony. A row of men lounged in the shade of the hotel porch farther down. Kingmead stepped into the saddle and turned that way. Here was another situation he had long known he must meet. The reins lay slack in his left hand; he slouched in the saddle and appeared to drowse as the horse slowly carried him toward the saloon. But his roving eyes took in every movement along that hot and silent street, and his right arm lay limp by his side.

As he came abreast the saloon, the doors of the place swung wide to reveal a figure Kingmead had never forgotten. Ruby Lusk stepped through, immense frame dipping with the awkward stride of his stubby legs. Ruby's hat was pushed far back and the sun glowed and glistened on his coppery face. Behind him walked Elmo Starrett, flushed and nervous. Kingmead turned the pony and halted, sitting immobile in the saddle, eyes half shut. Absolute stillness had come to the street; nothing seemed to move save Lusk and Starrett, and presently they too came to a halt in the soft dust. Lusk spat a cigarette from his flat lips and squinted upward. And he had ceased to smile.

"How, Ruby."

"Hello there, Hugh. Heard yuh was back."

"You look in good health, Ruby. Don't appear a day older."

"The climate," said Lusk with ominous significance, "agrees with me."

"It may be the company you keep, Ruby, and not the climate."

Ruby nodded. Kingmead noticed an increasing muddiness in the man's eyes; there was a dilation of the flat nostrils. These were signals—as a lion might lash its tail. The street grew hot and oppressive, more spectators lined the hotel porch. Elmo Starrett's sallow cheeks moved on a cud of tobacco. Kingmead looked at the youth and, not recognizing him, wondered at the flash of hatred that answered his inspection. Lusk turned his head toward the hotel porch and swung back to Kingmead quickly.

Hugh grinned. "Your orders don't cover a killin' in town, Ruby."

"What orders?"

"Orders Gesher gave you last night, Ruby." Hugh leaned forward. "You've always wanted to mount my horns pretty bad, haven't you?"

"Your card's a marked one," said Lusk, lips snapping back from his teeth. It was a mannerism that made a barbaric mask of his face. "Allus gave you credit for bein' sharp, Hugh. But it was a damn fool stunt to ride back."

Hugh's attention was again caught by Elmo Starrett's steady smirk of dislike. "Who's this smilin' gent with you, Ruby?"

"It's a name yuh might recall," muttered Lusk with a sudden grin. "Starrett's his monicker."

Kingmead's gravity deepened. "I'm sorry, kid. I reckon your feelin's toward me are plenty warm. Especially if you've been listenin' to Ruby much."

Venom spat out of Elmo's mouth. "I ain't able to face you on the street, fella! But, by God, I'm takin' to the rocks and if I ever get a shot at your back I'll take it same's I'd bag a ki-ote! That's a warnin'!" With that challenge he ran off to his horse, mounted, and raced out of town.

Ruby Lusk's barrel-like chest heaved outward. "Yuh called the turn, Hugh. I ain't mussin' up Sun Ford. Go on back to the hills and howl once. It's your last chance."

"I'm not runnin' this time, Ruby," replied Hugh. He swung away, presenting his back to the squat gunman. A row of sullen faces gaped at him from the porch. He passed on. Opposite the livery stable he drew rein again. There, half in the shade and half in the sun, stood Chiloquin Charley. His one-time partner had aged greatly since Kingmead last had seen him—aged and grown gaunt about the eyes.

"Well, by Judas Priest," cried Kingmead and dropped from the pony. "Man, how are you?" He strode up to Chiloquin and put out his hand.

Chiloquin shook his head. "Better ruffle up the dust,

Hugh. This town ain't your oyster. If it's the same to yuh, I won't shake."

Kingmead stared at Chiloquin Charley for a long interval. Then, without another word, he walked back to his pony and climbed up. For the first time that morning a hot and personal anger touched his nerves. He had ridden with this man, broken bread and shared secrets with him. He never looked back, but he heard a swift and subdued phrase overtake him.

"Don't get no wrong idees, Hugh. I give ev'body an even break. Mebbe yuh'll understand some later."

Kingmead raced south along the trail with that in his mind. Chiloquin had spoken for his ears alone. What was the matter with Chiloquin? Afraid of Lusk? He had never seen any man age so quickly. Chiloquin had once been a gay and rollicking partner.

This time Hugh Kingmead followed the trail. The morning was about gone, the freshness evaporated from the air. East and west the bench wavered with the heat and a fog dropped like a curtain across the southern horizon. Much had happened in those brief hours. As he put the miles to the rear, the conviction grew in his head that he had placed himself directly between the jaws of a trap. Eight years had solidified and increased Gesher's absolute sway. There had not been one man in Sun Ford glad to see him— not one willing to step out and shake his hand. Not one who had dared to do as much, even if willing. Against this solid wall what could he, Hugh Kingmead, hope to win?

He thought, *I'm marked. It's dodge and fight again. Supposin' they even left me alone—where would I start? How can I prove anything?*

One lone means was left him, doubtful and difficult. He could stalk Lusk and Lusk's men. Pick them up one by one and wring their necks until somebody squealed the secret of Ansel Starrett's death. He raised his head and swept the encroaching rock walls with a doubtful glance.

Such a way tasted bad on his tongue. He wasn't an Indian to burn the soles off a prisoner's feet. Supposing, leaving the torture out of it, he just captured them and held them back in the hills? Meanwhile the county would be up in arms and tracking him down.

"By Judas, I haven't got a trump in my hand," he muttered. "And no chips to bluff with. But—"

His thoughts were shattered. Across the droning air cracked a familiar sound. His horse broke pace and piled him up against the horn. The impact snapped his neck like the end of a whip and his hat sailed across the road. Out of plain instinct he laid the pony over against the ditch, fell from the saddle, and crouched beneath the shelter of a round boulder. A second bullet, coming down the slope, plowed into the shale rock three feet away.

The ambusher was somewhere up the bench side, cached behind a convenient shoulder of outcrop. And evidently in a sweat to finish off this chore. A third bullet ricocheted from his protecting rock. Another threw dust in his face. He constricted himself and weathered a barrage of lead that ran six shots, paused, and ran six more. His horse dropped without a sound, caught behind the ears. After that the firing stopped and nothing marred the shimmering silence. Kingmead listened for a telltale crunch of boots, one eye fixed on the blood puddling around his pony's head. Quite slowly, he turned his body to one side and raised his chin above the protection in time to see his ambusher ducking up the slope and toward a clump of pine trees.

Kingmead jumped from his covert and scrambled in pursuit, gun out. Once the man stopped, turned, and raised his rifle for another shot. It was too long a range. Kingmead dropped and waited until the other gave ground once more. The sweat rolled down his face and the rising dust choked him. Through this uncomfortable film he saw the ambusher reach the trees and dive through. Kingmead clawed at the loose rubble, reached the solid footing of a boulder, and stopped to wipe his face.

At that particular moment, and from an entirely different point of the compass, another gun raised the echoes. Hugh Kingmead dropped as if he were dead. The first ambusher reappeared from the pines and set up a fresh fusillade.

Chapter Five

GESHER STRIKES

Beyond dark, nine full hours later, Hugh Kingmead stumbled up to the line cabin and wearily confronted Izee Beulah and another of the old-time partners, Rube Mitchell. Izee exploded a single question. "Where in hell you been, Hugh?"

Rube, who was a giant of a man, six feet six in his stockings, loomed closer and gripped Hugh by the arm. "Kid, yuh didn't want none of us to come yet. Me, I couldn't wait. Wish it was light. Would like to see your face."

Hugh dropped on his haunches. "Rube, you old wampus cat! You boys ain't got any more business in this mess than a cockroach in soup. My pony's down on the trail, shot dead. I been in a scrap. Climbed over thirty thousand acres to get out of it. Who—I don't know who. Couple of fellows, both serious-minded. Skin's all scraped off my stomach, I've been that near to the ground. Didn't dare move till dark. Then I started walkin'."

"Didn't get either fellow, huh?" asked Izee in a matter-of-fact voice.

"Nope."

"That explains something," muttered Izee. "And queers something else."

"What are you mumbling about?" demanded Hugh, lighting a cigarette.

"Bad news, kid," explained Izee. "Rube and I come here around noon. We waited till dark and then, not hearin' nothin' from yuh, we got awful worried. So I rode down into Sun Ford after dark. Hell's loose from its picket. Three posses out in the hills. Yuh see, they found your hoss in the road and your hat near by."

"What of it?" Hugh inquired. "Since when does a dead horse make a murder?"

"Ain't the horse," replied Izee. He cleared his throat and said in an uneasy voice, "It's Elmo Starrett. He's been killed. They found his gun, his hat, and a sprinklin' o' blood on the shale rock by the hairpin bend o' the river."

Silence. Hugh suddenly rose, lit a match, and held it up to his partners' faces. "You cockeyed idiots, what makes you think I killed him?"

"Didn't say that," protested Izee weakly. "Didn't say it. Be good riddance if you had, but—"

"Oh, shut up! You're trying to back out of the hole. Listen, it fits too perfect. Same old rig that got me in trouble last time. My horse and, by the sufferin' Moses, my hat! That's a second time they figure to hang me on a Stetson. Where'd they find Elmo's body?"

"Ain't found it," said Rube Mitchell, with ill-concealed relief. "It looked to've been dragged acrost the ground some yards and then toted off on a hoss. Say, it shore does sound funny, don't it? Yuh left that neck o' the woods about twilight, huh? Which was near the time the news came into Sun Ford. Awful close connection there."

"So Elmo was shootin' at me?" mused Hugh Kingmead. "Like to know the other gent's name. I guess I could make a stab at it. Sure it's rigged. That's their way of putting me in the red. The woods will be full of posses from now on."

"We got to get out of here," decided Izee Beulah. "South into the brush. I'll pick up the rest of the boys—"

"Listen," interrupted Hugh, "I'll be damned if I'm going to drag you fellows into this mess. It means a rope or a gunshot for every gent connected with me. You go back and mind your—"

"Rube," grunted Izee, "I'd like to punch his nose."

Rube Mitchell's shoulders rose and fell in the darkness, as if he were hitching up his pants. "You go plumb straight to hell, Hugh Kingmead. It's our fight. I been waitin' to bust this county on its ear for eight seasons. Now I'm gonna. You shut up."

"All right. I warned you boys. Now you'll have to fight my style. We're not moving from here until they find us. First, I want to borrow one of your ponies. Next, you fellows skin back and collect the gang, get a pile of grub and plenty of ammunition. Meet me here in three-four hours."

"Where you goin'?" asked Izee.

Kingmead took a few moments before answering. His cigarette gleamed brightly. Higher up in the hills a coyote howled. He cleared his throat. "It may sound foolish to you, but I'm riding down to the Double Arrow S and tell Helena Starrett I didn't kill her brother."

"It don't sound foolish," objected Izee. "It is foolish. They's apt to be a pile o' men there. A couple of the crew anyhow. And that gal will give you away like a shirt full o' fleas. Your best bet is not to get away from us any more."

"I'm going," replied Hugh, and rose. "You two bust along and carry out the specifications. Meet me here later."

"Take my animal," grunted Rube. "I'll straddle behind Izee."

Kingmead found Rube's horse and mounted. Izee muttered a dire warning as he rode by, but Rube Mitchell's cheerful and unprintable cursing rose softly into the night. "Fly at it, Hugh. They can't match us nohow. I been wantin' to set this county on its ear." Hugh spurred down the slope.

History was repeating itself. A dead man in the hills and Hugh Kingmead's hat lying in the road. Lusk was in this, no doubt of it. And behind Lusk stood Gesher. Well, let them try the old trick again. If he ever got caught and was put up for trial, he knew that this time there would be no hung jury. Gesher was too powerful. But why all this trouble to cook up a charge against him? Gesher had ordered him to be tracked down and shot in the hills. Now it looked as if the man wanted to go through an empty legal ceremony and let the county do the killing. Gesher used the safest tools first.

"They'll never catch me until I'm ready to be caught," he mumured, picking up the lights of the Double Arrow S ranch-house. "But I want that girl to know—"

He paused at the road gate. No horses stood in front of the house porch, nobody moved about the place. He rode through, circled, and halted again deep in the shadows of a shed. Dropping to the ground, he crossed the yard to the porch and, not exactly pleased to be imitating a Peeping Tom, looked through a window. Helena Starrett sat on a divan, reading a black book. She had been crying, he saw, and the sight aroused the reckless fighting instinct he had suppressed all during his return. He moved to the door, knocked once, and opened it, sliding through quickly.

He expected a tongue lashing. He expected her to run back and summon help from the bunkhouse. He expected anything but the quiet, straight look she gave him. There was no anger in it, no trace of the hatred she had heaped upon him during the morning. It took him so much off guard that for several moments he leaned against the door.

"You're not wise to come here," she said. The book closed, a white finger marking a page. "There's fifty men looking for you, Hugh Kingmead."

"I said I'd stay away, Miss. I'm breakin' that promise. I want you to know I didn't touch your brother. You may or may not believe it, but there's my word."

"I believe you."

"I hadn't expected you to," murmured Hugh Kingmead. The lamplight glimmered on her black hair and made a silhouette of her small, square shoulders. This girl was unforgettable, not so much for her beauty as for the sturdy stuff she was made of. He had seen her thrice in the last few days, once smiling and provocative, once pitched to the highest note of emotion, and now touched with sadness. In whatever mood, Hugh Kingmead felt the clean and full freedom of her mind. She was no drawing-room belle; she could fight, and she was not afraid to let herself go when she was so inclined. But she stood up under the stress of trouble, she wasn't weak.

"I know you hadn't," said she. "I didn't want to believe you either, Hugh Kingmead. All the way home today I tried to make you out a liar. But—but I don't think you can lie. No, it wasn't only that. I have been looking over the Double Arrow S ledger this afternoon. Something has happened to this ranch. My two punchers say Elmo sold stock to Gesher. More stock has been lost—rustled. Lusk was here last night and gambled with Elmo until daylight. Now Elmo's gone—oh, I can't think, after seeing and knowing all this, that you're to blame." Her hands gripped the book. Her voice ran up to a singing pitch, anxious and appealing. "What do you think they've done with Elmo? What did they do to you?"

"Somebody tried to shoot me off the road," said Hugh. He lied gravely. "Some of Lusk's outfit. That's why my hat and horse were discovered. Same old trick they pulled on me the other time. Don't you understand the politics of this county?"

"Gesher?" It was a faint whisper.

"Yeah. I—"

She turned her head. The silence of the night was broken by a distant drumming. Instantly she was on her feet and moving back toward the kitchen door. "Come quick."

He followed her into the kitchen. It was quite dark; as he stood against the wall her hand touched him and the faint fragrance of her clothing disturbed the swift run of his thoughts. "It's probably a posse. Go out the back way and run to the hills. I—I believe you, Hugh."

"That's the second break I've had in forty-eight hours," said he, checking an impulse to touch her.

The drumming drew nearer and became a confused pounding of hoofs. A voice challenged the shadows and somebody stumbled away from the bunkhouse and around to the front of the place. "What," whispered Helena Starrett, "was the first break?"

"Five of my old partners are up on the bench waiting for me. They'll go the limit."

Her voice was muffled. "I didn't want to believe you. I do now. Go on—and keep out of their reach."

"I think it'd be a good idea to listen in on this party," he decided. "It might give me something to work on." The horsemen were in the front yard; phrases seeped into the kitchen. "You haven't got much protection here now. Listen, the boys and me are camped up on the east bench at Number One line cabin of the old Sawhorse outfit. Remember that?"

"Yes—be still now." She slipped away through the kitchen door. In the moment it stood open Hugh Kingmead saw men filing in the front way. Gesher and Lusk were foremost. Then he was in the complete darkness again with his ear laid against the door panel. Gesher's tinder-dry words carried distinctly to him.

"Evenin', Miss Starrett. Want to express my concern and sympathy over what's happened. Don't trouble yourself with the result. We'll have Kingmead in jail before dark tomorrow. He's run his head into a noose. A criminal always comes back."

"Are you very sure, Mr. Gesher, it was Kingmead?" countered the girl.

"You're the last person to doubt it, ma'am," said Gesher, slightly admonitory. "His history is ample evidence."

An interval of silence followed in which Kingmead heard a heavy body cruising about the room. It approached the kitchen door and seemed to halt there. Kingmead's arm dropped to his gun. Gesher spoke again, clearing his throat. "This, maybe, will be a surprise to you. As long as your brother lived I didn't feel like pressin' him. Now, I've got to protect myself. Y' see, I hold his I.O.U.'s for a considerable sum."

"How did you get them?" inquired Helena Starrett with a note of angry distrust.

"Your brother played cards with some o' the boys. They wanted cash, so I bought the notes from them. A matter of obligation to me. Elmo would've made the amount good. But since he's gone I've got to protect myself. The sum will about cover the assessed value of this ranch."

"I expected to hear something like that," said the girl, and Kingmead was surprised at her calmness. "But you understand that I am not paying any poker debts."

"The law provides they're legal debts," rasped Gesher. "If you ain't willing to pay them, I reckon I'll have to protect myself by puttin' my men on this ranch to manage it."

"So? Have you forgotten that I own half of the Double Arrow S, Mr. Gesher? If Elmo gave you I.O.U.'s above his share of the property, that is your loss. You cannot touch my interest by a dollar."

The heavy body moved slowly away from the kitchen door. Gesher grew sharper. "A Starrett always paid his debts."

"Honest ones," parried Helena.

"Well, if that's your stand I guess I'll have to lose a little. Your father wouldn't have approved such a denial of obligations. But I will insist on half of the ranch. And to protect myself I'll leave Mr. Lusk and a set of hands to cover my interests."

"Let's see those I.O.U.'s."

Kingmead shifted his body and waited. Some of the party grunted. Ruby Lusk's growl cut across this. "Yuh ain't sleepin' here. This is my room."

"Is it?" Helena asked. "I don't suppose I can keep you from moving in, but there's a bunkhouse out back. Not one of you'll step inside this house. Here's your I.O.U.'s, Mr. Gesher. You tricked and used my brother very easily, didn't you?"

"That ain't kindly," said Gesher. "I'm protectin' myself. Lusk, send your men to the bunkhouse. You find a room here for yourself."

"I forbid that."

Gesher's answer was curt and unfriendly. "It ain't in your power, Miss Starrett, to forbid anything. What I own I manage my own way."

"You don't own this, Gesher."

"It amounts to that. I bid you good evenin'."

Boots tramped in and out. Kingmead heard Helena excuse herself and walk toward the kitchen door. He drew back as it opened, seeing Lusk and Gesher talking earnestly at the front. In the ensuing darkness the girl spoke hurriedly. "Don't waste time. Slip off before they get settled."

"You can't stay in the house with Lusk," protested Hugh. "How about me sleepin' in here?"

"No! You would be caught by daylight! Why put yourself in their hands? If you are going to fight, you must get away."

"My Lord, girl, don't you know anything about Ruby Lusk?"

"More," she whispered, "than you think. But I've got two loyal punchers with me. Go on now."

Her arm grazed his chest and he was half pushed across the kitchen to an open door. "Be careful!" she warned him.

He stopped a moment. "Have one of your boys saddle a horse on the quiet and leave it somewhere. If this proposition gets beyond you, ride up to the line camp."

"Be careful, Hugh."

She was gone, leaving him with the memory of her voice and the pressure of her fingers on his arm. The bunkhouse blazed with light, and figures walked across the yellow beam. He heard men laughing, and he heard men quarreling. He ducked through the kitchen exit and, hugging the shadows of the house, came to its corner. Lusk's domineering tones reached him faintly and for a moment he debated going back. He would have turned save that he heard Gesher's dry farewell at the front and a moment later made out the man's horse cantering away, bound townward alone. Kingmead bent over and went across into the heavy trees where his pony waited. He led the animal out past the sheds and corrals and then, at a discreet distance, flung himself into the saddle and raced recklessly to the northward.

The cold air fanned his cheeks, the stars were dim and remote. To his left lay the twisted surface of the river, dully luminous. He was on the trail a moment, but only for a moment. The river made an oxbow, turning the trail temporarily away from the direction of Sun Ford. Kingmead spurred into the water and started across; his pony sank out of footing and swam downstream, touched gravelly shelving, and clambered up a stiff bank. There was no trail on this side but Kingmead, knowing the country of old, swung through and around the cottonwood clumps, skirted tributary washes, and crossed a small butte. The road was far behind. Down the butte's slope he raced. He came to an area of rock and traced it slowly, the impatience rising in him at the delay. Passing this, he plunged into a grove of stunted pines, threaded an arroyo, and reached a clear meadow. The river once more. He had traveled two miles to its three. Once again he forded, this time with caution, and halted in the trail to Sun Ford.

The night's breeze came out of the west. Recognizing this, he crossed to the east side of the trail, thus keeping the smell of his horse from going down the road to warn any approaching beast. Before he was settled he heard the rhythmic thump of Gesher's horse coming on. Gesher was a dangerous man, a supremely confident man to be riding the night alone at a time like this.

Kingmead drew his gun and moved nearer the road. He had a vague view of horse and rider; then Gesher was abreast him. A quirt flailed down. Gesher's dry voice crackled, his body swayed back as Kingmead shot against him. Saddle touched saddle, both horses reared, pulled apart, and closed again. Kingmead's arm fell like a sledge across Gesher's gun arm; when the horses next drew apart Gesher was down in the dust and Kingmead was on top, bearing all his weight on the other's skinny frame.

Gesher put up a short, tremendously vicious fight. His arms battered Kingmead's head, his nails furrowed the big man's face. He squirmed, trying to catch Kingmead with his knees. The latter redoubled the pressure. "Cut it out, Loren."

"Kingmead!"

"Yeah. Now cut it out or I'll knock you dizzy."

Resistance ended. Kingmead hauled the man upright and shucked his coat down from his shoulders. That pinioned Gesher's arms.

"You terrible fool!" Gesher panted. "Keep your hands out of my pockets!"

Kingmead found a long leather folder. Opening it, he felt a sheaf of paper. "If these are Starrett's I.O.U.'s, Loren, I'm going to relieve you of 'em."

"Highway robbery, huh?"

"What's a little thing like that to a killer like me, Loren? I told you not to underestimate me."

"They'll be back in my hands by tomorrow night. And you with 'em."

"If you talk like that, Loren, I'm apt to put a match to this wallet. Listen—you're plain hydrophobia to me and I'm a fool to let you go. If I only had a place to put you, maybe I wouldn't let you go. Absorb this, I'm not stealin' these I.O.U.'s. I'm borrowin' 'em. You'll get the whole mess back, or their approximate value. But if you don't draw Lusk and his thugs off the Double Arrow S in twenty-four hours, you never will see this wallet again. Bite into that. I'm pullin' one of your stingers. Pretty soon I'll pull some more. Maybe it didn't sink in when I told you I was back to stay. One of us goes under. Now get on your pony and strike for town."

Kingmead unbuckled Gesher's holster and patted him for additional weapons. Gesher rose and limped to his horse. In the saddle he tarried and Kingmead saw, dimly, a false movement of reins. "Don't try to reach Lusk, Loren. I'll be waiting here a little while. Go on to town."

"You're soon dead, Kingmead."

"All of us die too soon, Loren. Travel."

Gesher vanished down the road. Kingmead thoughtfully climbed the slope. Maybe he shouldn't have allowed Gesher to go free. But he wanted to show Gesher he wasn't afraid. Anyhow, the kidnaping business wouldn't help him win over public sentiment. And he knew that unless he did this he could never hope to live in the county.

When he reached the line cabin he found that his partners hadn't returned yet. Going inside, he lit a match and inspected the wallet. The I.O.U.'s were folded together. Some bills and a few stray papers were with them. Kingmead tallied up the sum of those I.O.U.'s and was unpleasantly surprised. "Enough to start a bank. Gesher played that Elmo kid down to his socks. And murdered him. Well, a poker debt is a debt. But this money was won crooked. Still, it's money. Gesher'll get something in trade for these John Henry's. No more'n my conscience will allow, which is about a cent on the dollar."

He went outside. It wasn't safe carrying the wallet around. Not only that, but he'd been toting too much cash of his own. Anything might happen. Down the slope fifty yards from the line cabin, he rolled aside a rock weighing better than two hundred pounds, cached his money and the I.O.U.'s, and returned to the cabin to wait.

Away down the slope he heard the rustling of sage bushes.

After the departure of Kingmead from the kitchen, Helena Starrett returned to the living-room to find Ruby Lusk sprawled comfortably on the divan. Helena had seen this man, at intervals, since she was a small girl, and though he bore a sinister reputation, she never had felt a fear of him. Perhaps it was the smile he habitually wore, or the rumbling and seeming joviality of his voice. Tonight it was different. Here he lay, watching her out of his muddy eyes, working his crushed lips across his yellow teeth. And when he lifted one of his immense arms and twitched his bull neck, fear swept over her like a shock of electricity. She walked to a far corner of the room, feeling the impact of his steady, narrow inspection. And she squared her shoulders and turned on him.

"You've got no right here, Lusk. Go on out to the bunkhouse."

"Owners sleep in the big house, Helena."

"Don't use my name! You're not an owner."

"It amounts to that," said Ruby Lusk, mimicking Gesher's statement. "Listen, girl, you ought to know Gesher an' me by now. What he gets he keeps. What he tells me to do, I shore do it."

"Are you trying to drive me away?"

He lolled back, enjoying this scene. "Gesher's mighty set in his ways. An' he's wanted this rancho some long time. He's patient. He can wait." He stopped to see the effect of this on the girl. "Your old man never liked me, did he? Shore would've hurt him to see me in here. Every dawg has a couple of good barks at the moon. I'm doin' it now. Told yuh last night I waited for yuh to grow up, didn't I? When yuh goin' to marry me?"

"So you fight women!" she shot back. "Is there nothing you don't do?"

His big barrel chest moved to a soundless laugh. "I don't herd sheep."

The girl walked past him, fighting against the trembling muscles of her body. Her room was up the stairs but she went directly to the door of the lower bedroom—Elmo's room. On the threshold of that room she turned. He hadn't moved, but there was the same intent look upon his face she had noted the previous night. The firelight streamed over his battered cheeks; he was a picture of evil, he was an animal unconscious of any moral responsibility. And not until she closed the door did the full extent of her danger dawn on her. She turned the key softly and crossed the room. A window, the sash already raised, opened out to the rear. She drew aside the curtains, listening.

He was up on his feet, cruising around the front room. She marked each backward and forward path he made and at each approach she grew as cold as ice. Each time it seemed he came a little closer; the heavy tread stopped and with the cessation of sound she forgot to breathe. The knob of the door turned, there was a faint squealing of the hinges, and she saw in her mind his powerful shoulders pressing against the barrier. What good was a door against Ruby Lusk?

"Pray God—" she murmured and lifted herself out of the window. Her shoes woke a small echo as they touched the ground and it seemed to swell and warn the world of her flight. To stay on this ranch longer was impossible. Nor did she dare to try to find the two loyal hands. Only one thing she could do. So she ran lightly across the yard toward the barn. One horse was always stabled against an emergency. That had been a habit of her father's. How could he ever have dreamed of an emergency like this one?

She fell against the ground, feeling the terrific pounding of her heart. The bunkhouse door opened and a man came out and walked slowly toward the main house. He passed within ten yards of her, so close that she heard his breathing. Then he turned into the porch and she got up and went on. On into the darkness of the barn. A bridle and saddle were on the pegs and swiftly she put them on the horse. "Easy, boy," she whispered. Leading him away, she sprang up and turned toward the corrals. Around them, around the meadow, and past the house to the Sun Ford trail. And although every nerve and muscle prompted her to set the horse into a mad gallop, she bit into her lip and restrained the impulse for a half mile. Then she fled into the night; and it seemed to her that a thousand men were in pursuit.

She knew every foot of this ground, she had ridden it a thousand times. Yet some time after she left the main trail and started the climb toward the line cabin a panic overtook her. The night was full of weird shapes, sinister with pursuing echoes. And though she had never yet been lost and never yet let darkness prey on her imagination, a call rose out of her throat and beat up along the hill. Instantly she was sorry for it. She stopped, thinking she heard the sagebrush rustle below and the clack of a hoof. But she could make nothing definite of it; so she went on until a definite shape floated in front of her and Hugh Kingmead's low, comforting voice broke the terror.

"Who is it?"

"Hugh!"

"Yeah, I thought it was you. Poor kid, I ought never have left." He rode beside her, laying his arm on her shoulder. "It's hell when they fight women. I'm chalkin' that up. And when payday comes for Gesher and Lusk they'll sweat it out."

"I've never been afraid," murmured the girl, "never until—"

"—until now," he finished. "Lord bless you, it ain't anything to be ashamed of. That fellow Lusk makes me creepy sometimes. We'll ride to the cabin. The boys ain't back yet. Hark—"

They stopped. Kingmead's arm pressed her down into the saddle with a sudden, savage power. Out of the foreground and out of the flanking distance came definite sounds. Before he could draw his gun, Ruby Lusk's rumbling voice challenged him. "Stay right there, Hugh. Don't want to start shootin', do yuh? Wouldn't want us to lay lead around the girl?" His soft, mirthless chuckle palpitated through the shadows. "I smelled somethin' damn queer, Helena, when yuh took the downstairs bedroom. It ain't your usual bunk." Then the pleasantry deserted him. He snarled like an infuriated animal. "Let me hear that gun drop, Kingmead! Give up!"

The girl was crying. "Hugh—I gave you away! I didn't know—"

"Don't worry none," muttered Hugh. Lusk's shape slid nearer. He heard others narrow the ring around him. "Don't worry. All the aces ain't out of the deck yet. You win, Ruby. What's it to be?"

"Throw the gun. Gesher's changed his mind. Wants yuh in the jug. County's goin' to do the hanging. I'd like to do it myself, but orders go. Throw that gun."

"Listen," warned Hugh. "The girl goes with me. She stays at the hotel, understand? Keep your dirty carcass away from her."

"That goes," agreed Lusk. "I only scared her out of the house to see what she had up her sleeve. She'll like me sometime. I can wait."

"If you break that word, Ruby," said Hugh, words falling solemnly outward, "I'll see you die in torment."

Ruby laughed ironically. "Throw the gun."

Hugh Kingmead obeyed the order. Lusk's party closed in. Hugh was searched and his arms tied. There was an abrupt order from the burly renegade and the party struck down the bench and rode silently into Sun Ford. The girl dropped off at the hotel. And shortly before dawn, Hugh Kingmead was behind bars.

Chapter Six

THE MOB AT NIGHT

IN THIS BARREN SECOND-STORY CELL, with its plastered walls bearing the autographs of a hundred former residents, Hugh Kingmead slept. He had been on the move for twenty hours, he had stretched his physical equipment to a limit it had not reached in eight years. In the old days this would have meant nothing; he had piled night on day and day on night then with only the traditional three-hour sleep between. But the East had sapped him of that resiliency; he was not yet whipped up to the splendid shape of his earlier years. And so he slumbered while the outside world resounded to the news of his capture and events marched toward some tremendous and tragic climax.

At dawn the restaurant's clanging triangle beat faintly on his consciousness, like the fragment of a dream. Other sounds troubled him—the hollow echo of a man's voice upraised in the street below, the drip of water, the shuffle of boots, the clinking of keys, and a sharp order. Then he was awake. The nooning sun burned through the grated window and made a checkered pattern on the casing. Loren

Gesher's sand-colored face was beyond the door bars, with the expression of tight and hard pleasure upon it.

Kingmead sat erect and planted his feet on the floor. "Hello, Loren. Poor time to be sleepin', ain't it! But I'm not the chap I used to be. None of us are. You're not either. Worry's got you all screwed up in a knot. Eight years saps a fellow, and there ain't much left of you to sap. Ever consider, Loren, that some day we die?"

"What," asked Gesher in a dead-level voice, "did you do with my pocketbook?"

"That's what your jailer wanted to know last night," replied Hugh, grinning. "Or if he didn't know about the pocketbook he sure was inquisitive about what I carried. Guess I must've dropped it in the struggle."

"What did you do with it?" demanded Gesher, more sharply.

"You damn fool, I cached it, and all that was in it."

Gesher took hold of the bars with his bony fingers and he stood on his toes, shoulders rising. Kingmead saw the man's features freeze with a kind of paralytic stroke and he knew that Gesher was racked by a tremendous fury— the fury evoked by helplessness. He was only a single straw across Loren Gesher's path; Gesher might crush him instantly. Yet for all of that, Hugh Kingmead had checked Gesher, had disarranged the latter's plans for the moment. And since this was almost the first time in eight years anyone had openly challenged Gesher's ruthless march toward power, it was bound to arouse all the accumulated venom and tyranny in the man's nature. Kingmead got to his feet and walked toward the door.

"I told you not to underestimate me. You're a shriveled-up little centipede and you've got a sting that's about fatal. But you ain't stung me yet, Loren. I'll break your back before this thing's finished."

Gesher's shoulders fell. He turned and walked along the hall and down the stairs without a word. Kingmead, bothered more than he cared to admit, rolled a cigarette and tramped the four corners of the room. *There's poison in that gent,* he thought, *and I'm a direct heir to all the misfortune he's cooking up. What was the idea of me talking so cocksure? Right now I'm jammed up against two certain facts. Either they'll hold another trial and hook me with a rigged jury or else there'll be a mob break in here and decorate a tree with my carcass. Gesher's playing for one or the other thing to happen. Either way, he's clear of legal responsibility.*

It was time for dinner, but no dinner came to him. The town grew noisier with the passing moments, the sun slid away from his window and the small cubicle was filled with a stifling heat. Kingmead went to the window and looked out upon a back alley, to find a man slouched idly in an abandoned wagon seat. The fellow looked upward and, seeing Kingmead, patted his holster. Kingmead retreated and tapped the plastered walls. What was all the talking and all the shuffling down below supposed to indicate?

Izee and the boys will know where I am, he mused. *But it won't do 'em much good. Not while it's light. Something's up.*

Men climbed the stairs and clustered in front of the door—the jailer, a gentleman with a sheriff's star, and three flint-faced bystanders. The lock was turned and the door opened.

"Come on out," said the sheriff. "We're taking you to court."

"Doesn't this county furnish meals to its guests?" parried Kingmead, passing through.

"Yuh won't miss it much in the long run," said the sheriff.

"And the condemned ate no hearty breakfast," quipped Kingmead. The jailer went ahead of Hugh, the sheriff and the others followed behind. They crossed the hot street to the weather-beaten courthouse and in that short passage a crowd of twenty men closed in. The sheriff grunted a warning, Hugh entered the place and stopped by the judicial bench. Ruby Lusk elbowed through the gathering spectators, Loren Gesher sat in a chair close by, as if he had been awaiting this scene. And when the judge appeared through a rear door Hugh Kingmead saw a sharp glance pass between the two men. Someone spoke at his shoulder; he turned to see the man who twice had tried to convict him of murder and was again to make the attempt—Prosecuting Attorney Best.

Whisky had damped much of the man's vigor, that was plain to Kingmead. And eight years had printed heavy lines on his face. He threw back his head and stared dourly at Kingmead, a queer light flickering in his hazel eyes. Kingmead thought the man had gone to seed; there was about him the air of the political hanger-on and the unscrupulous partisan. "This time, Kingmead, I've got you hooked. I tried to send you to hell twice. This time it works."

"Loren Gesher's been pretty kind to you, Best," drawled Hugh. "He's kept your nest feathered plenty warm, hasn't he?"

Best dropped his voice to a murmur. "I've always had sense enough to see the buttered side of the bread. Why don't you see it?" Then he turned to the judge and his voice took on the hard and professionally confident tone of his office. "Y'honor, we propose to try the prisoner for the murder of Elmo Starrett. At this preliminary hearing, if the court pleases—"

"Got a lawyer?" interrupted the court, directing a skinny finger toward Hugh.

"No need in throwing money away," said Hugh, "on a case like this. I would like to know how a man can be tried for murder when the alleged dead person hasn't been produced? Who claims that young Starrett is dead?"

"I claim it," snapped Best. "There is no profit in hedging on technicalities. When the proper time comes we will produce—" His voice trailed off to a nod in the direction of Ruby Lusk. Loren Gesher had risen and was now whispering something in the burly renegade's ear. Lusk nodded toward the judge. "We'll have Elmo Starrett's body here by tomorrow mornin'. I know where Kingmead hid it."

The judge squinted across the upper rim of his glasses and thought upon the case carefully. "Can't book him for the demise of Elmo Starrett without producin' said Starrett's body. However, we can hold him for investigation. Meanwhile, Best, why not change the charge to murder of Colonel Ansel Starrett? The old indictment against him still holds."

"We will do that then," agreed Best. There was a noticeable stir in the courtroom. Kingmead saw Chiloquin Charley's brooding face in a corner. And near the door he discovered Helena Starrett. All this was prearranged. It sounded like a rehearsal. The judge cleared his throat.

"Return prisoner to jail," said he. "Bring your case to court at nine in the mornin'. Adjourned."

Recrossing the street to the jail, Hugh Kingmead was aware of the waxing hostility. And he knew that as the afternoon passed and the men of the county came in to drink and to rehearse the old story there would be a slow fanning of this hostility until it reached a pitch of recklessness. A word and a flourish—and Sun Ford would be in the hands of a mob. Inside his cell again he debated this thoroughly.

This town is Gesher's, body and breeches. So's Best, the judge, the sheriff, and the whole bunch of them down to the lowest drunken skunk in it. This end of the county is Gesher's—owned outright, stolen, trespassed, leased, or browbeaten. For thirty years or more he's been building the machine and it's damn near perfect right now. There's honest men here, but they're saying nothing at all. They can't say anything. What chance have I got!

Well, he had one slim hope. If he could make those honest folks see they had a respectable fighting chance to overthrow Gesher's organization, he might make a stand.

He walked around the cell again, speculatively tapping the plaster. *I passed a bet when I let Loren go. Should've buried him with the wallet. Between now and dark I've got to get out of here. No matter how much skin I lose in the transaction, I've got to break away.*

He stopped his inspection of the walls and sat on the bunk's edge. Somebody came up the stairs, talking to the jailer. Presently Chiloquin Charley's face appeared beyond the bars. The jailer surveyed the cell and walked away, advising Chiloquin not to waste his time. Chiloquin waited until the jailer was out of hearing, slouched against the bars, a somber, moody figure. Once this man had been a partner of Kingmead's. Yet here he stood, so trusted by the Gesher partisans that the jailer left him alone at the cell door.

Kingmead rolled a cigarette. "Chiloquin," he murmured, "I've been singin' the same song all afternoon. Eight years is a long time, isn't it?"

"Some," muttered Chiloquin Charley.

"Folks change. There's something eatin' the liver out of you, Chiloquin. The devil's stared in your face, old-timer, and he's tipped you off to what hell looks like."

Chiloquin stood as still as death and a film of sweat spread across his forehead. "Damn yuh, Hugh! Yuh got a gift o' readin' gents. Yuh always did have it. Let me alone —cut that palaver. What made yuh come back, anyhow? It was all settled; it was cut an' dried till yuh rides through Sun Ford. Why kick up old dust—why raise old ghosts?"

"What do you get for holdin' Gesher's cards?" asked Hugh. "I remember a time, Chiloquin, when you and I rode together—"

"Cut that out. Who said I held Gesher's cards? But

things was settled. Yo're only diggin' into old graves. I ain't slept an hour since yuh got here. Listen—I followed the trail with you boys. If I went another way it ain't because—"

He stopped and turned his head down the hallway. Kingmead had never seen a man so grimly earnest. But Chiloquin, on the very edge of a revelation, caught himself. He put his cheeks against the bars, speaking above a whisper. "They can't hang yuh for killin' Elmo Starrett unless they produce the kid's carcass in court. And they can't produce his carcass unless they kill him."

Hugh Kingmead rose and came to the door. "What's your hole card, Chiloquin? I don't get you. Not at all. What do you know about Elmo Starrett?"

"I want to see you clear, Hugh," muttered Chiloquin. His eyes were like live coals and his cheek muscles made white ridges against his sun-blackened skin. "Mebbe I ain't got as bad a heart as this town and county figgers. He ain't dead, I'm tellin' it. But yuh got to get clear. If they don't hang yuh for Elmo, they'll hang yuh for old Colonel Ansel. And yuh didn't kill him, either."

"What do you know about that scrape?"

"Plenty," grunted Chiloquin. Once more he cast a wary glance down the corridor. His arm went inside his coat and came out with a forty-five. He poked it through the bars into Kingmead's open fists. "Plant that. Tonight when the sher'ff comes in with supper—"

He slid back from the bars and moved off. Kingmead heard a last warning: "Don't go by the back door. They got it watched. Front way—to the first alley."

Kingmead listened to the man's retreat down the stairs. He heard a rumble of conversation below and a scraping of chairs. Quite thoughtfully he cached the gun under the blankets of the bunk and went to the rear window. They had changed guards out there—another puncher sat in the abandoned buggy seat. The sun's slanting rays were slowly marching farther away from the buildings. Dust rose out of a corral, short and profane words snapped across the dry air, and still farther along the prairie shimmered beneath the afternoon's heat. Kingmead retreated to the bunk and rolled a cigarette. If Elmo Starrett wasn't dead, then some of Gesher's men must be holding him out there on the bench. And Lusk had told the judge he would produce a dead man's body by morning. Did they mean to kill Elmo Starrett in cold blood in order to make a case against him?

Gesher would do it, decided Hugh. *And Lusk's the man to carry out that kind of an order. But I don't fathom Chiloquin Charley.*

He knew that Chiloquin once had been a friend; then something had happened to Chiloquin. In this land, overborn by Gesher's iron hand, it took a strong man to resist the pressure to go wrong. There was a ceaseless interplay of threat and bribery and violence. Men were not inanimate. They didn't follow a straight line. They grew stronger or they crumbled. Eight years was a long time and Hugh Kingmead in returning had discovered that the old line of cleavage had tightened and extended and embraced those who once had been powerful enough to resist. Chiloquin was one of those.

But why had Chiloquin brought him a gun? Was it the old trick—to let him fight his way to the street that he might die by a bullet? Or had the memory of their former friendship stirred Chiloquin to this one act of betrayal of the sinister company he had joined? A man's heart was filled with obscure promptings; it was a dark chamber of doubt and pride and honor and deceit and loyalty. God alone knew what was in Chiloquin's heart, though Kingmead saw that his old comrade was on the rack.

Kingmead debated, so thoroughly involved with his thoughts that dusk came to the cell unobserved and the heat of day vanished. The echoes of the town came up in clearer, sharper waves. Presently it was dark and there was a crowd outside the jail. Kingmead rose and took the gun from under the bunk blankets. Standing in the middle of the cell, he heard the rising tone of the mob. A lantern's light winked through the rear window. He stirred and moved closer to the door. The noise of the mob sank to smaller dimensions and Hugh Kingmead, suddenly chilled by the full knowledge of his danger, recognized Helena Starrett's voice reasoning with the crowd.

There was a scraping of a heavy object on the jail roof; he retreated to a far corner and there in the heavy shadows he stood motionless, gun leveled across the room. Showdown was not far off; Judge Lynch rode in Sun Ford this night, a grim phantom ready to condemn and to execute. The cell was growing colder but Hugh Kingmead wiped sweat from his forehead and swore softly. He had never in his life feared a gun. But to be trampled and torn by a mob and then to be strangled by a rope and finished with a bullet while hanging with a knot under his left ear was a different matter.

Helena Starrett had been left at Sun Ford's hotel when Lusk arrived in town with his prisoner. She was dead tired, yet she could not sleep. For she had seen the glint of sinister triumph in Lusk's eyes and she knew what that meant for Hugh Kingmead. From her window she watched the men of the county come riding in during the hot morning and she marked them by name and by politics. Three-quarters of them belonged to one or the other of Gesher's numerous ranches and she realized that they came by command of their chief to pack the town and to sway opinion. Here and there she recognized a man who might be impartial, but they were few and they would not venture to oppose Gesher. When court time arrived she saw Hugh Kingmead cross the street heavily guarded and she hurried out. But she had no chance to speak to him.

There was always somebody in the room to block her way; she was under surveillance. Once she caught Hugh's eyes and in that single glance she tried to tell him she meant to stand by him, that his fortunes were her fortunes. And when she saw how he carried himself in the face of this peril a lump came to her throat and she dug her nails deep into the palms of her hands to keep back the tears. Hugh Kingmead was a man!

Later she tried to get the jailer to let her go up to the cell. He motioned her gruffly away and she returned to the hotel room. The long afternoon gave way to dusk, and in the deepening shadows she saw the crowd gathering around the jail and through the open window she made out the guttural rumble of their talk. It was general talk at first, but presently there was a spokesman and he was rehearsing the old history of Hugh Kingmead in words that were meant to inflame the temper of the gathering. Soon there would be a fatal phrase, a fatal move, and they would break into the jail. Nothing could stop them when that moment came. She turned from the window and went swiftly down and out of the hotel.

She had a dim and hopeless idea of finding a few men who would protect the jail. So she walked along the street, looking into the faces of those she passed. Down as far as the stable and across the back on the other side. She could not find one to trust. All that was left to her now was to speak up. They would listen—they had to listen. Repeating this to herself over and over, she crowded through the circle of men, feeling the weight of their glances, hearing their muttered phrases—phrases that brought the blood to her face. One of them tried to stop her; she knocked his arm away and came to the center of the group. Lusk was there, arms akimbo, his battered face grimly set. There was another man talking—some Gesher rider whose name she didn't know. He turned on her and marked her with an outstretched finger.

"There's the girl whose daddy and kid brother this Kingmead gent slaughtered. Now are you boys a-goin' to stand by an' see him wiggle clear again? No, by God!"

The swelling response frightened her, left her weak and trembling, drained the color from her cheeks. A lantern flashed brightly against her face and made her feel as if she were on the auction block. She heard herself speaking to them, words sounding remote and unreal.

"I have a right to say something. How do any of you know Hugh Kingmead killed my folks? What proof have you got—what proof strong enough to make you speak of lynching? Oh, it isn't right—it isn't right! What is law for? It isn't your place to judge and convict him. Don't you believe in giving a man a fair chance?"

The murmuring stopped and she thought she had reached their sense of justice. She thought so until Ruby Lusk moved forward a pace. The man said no word at all, but his scarred, uneven face wrinkled sardonically and his laugh echoed around the circle. Nothing more, yet it swept away whatever impression she might have made. Somebody back of her said, "Let's get this over with," and the circle wavered and grew smaller.

"Wait!" cried the girl. "If anybody should feel like having revenge, am I not the one? Who does it mean more to than myself? And up until yesterday I believed all the stories told about Hugh Kingmead. I wanted to see him brought to justice. But listen. No matter how good or how bad a man might be, do any of you honestly believe he'd return to kill my brother and leave exactly the same sort of evidence behind him? Would the most ignorant kind of a killer do that? Of course not. And what reason would he have for hurting Elmo?"

"Plenty," broke in a puncher at her side. "Doggone plenty, sister. Your kid brother told Kingmead he was out to get him. So Kingmead beat him to the draw."

She felt herself being pushed slowly backward. The crowd moved inexorably in the direction of the jail door. Desperately she fought against the tide.

"You boys know that doesn't make sense! Wait—wait until I tell you the rest of it. Last night Loren Gesher came to my house with all the I.O.U. notes Elmo had lost over the poker tables. How did he get them? What was the reason? Because he wanted the Double Arrow S. If you want to find who killed my folks, look nearer to Loren Gesher! I know most of you boys work for him, but why should you do his dirty chores? Don't you see he's behind all this—don't you see it only helps his hand if you lynch Hugh Kingmead? Don't be—"

Ruby Lusk raised an arm and in the lantern light his flat and bruised features ran together in an ugly, malevolent smear. "All right," he grunted. The open space was closed by crowding bodies. Helena beat against them with her fists and was struck in return. Somebody picked her up by the waist and she went whirling along the crowd, passed from hand to hand, the breath squeezed out of her. She screamed and the sound of it seemed to touch off the mob's fury. A hot hand slapped against her mouth, her hair was pulled down over her face, and then she was thrown out of the path of all those trampling feet—thrown violently against the sidewalk. She fell and ripped her arm across a loose nail.

Somebody pulled her farther away into the darkness and left her there. Her side hurt her and her lips were bruised. So she crouched, terror in her heart, while the jail door went crashing down and the mob fought up the stairway. She heard one protesting voice—it must have been the jailer's—but it was only a halfhearted protest and soon stilled. A table went over. Men were cursing, calling back through the second-story window. Iron beat against iron. A great challenge reverberated out of the place. "Come out, Kingmead!" Then there was a double explosion and the fury of the crowd swept down the stairs and into the street like the blast of a cyclone.

Kingmead, in the dark corner of the cell, heard Helena Starrett talking to the crowd. But he had only half an ear for it. Something else gripped his attention at the moment —a sound of shingles ripping above, the rasp of a saw biting into wood. At first it was faint and intermittent, coming down softly to him. Then as the crowd began to move and to give voice to its passions, those above abandoned their caution and tore into the roof. Plaster and lath showered from the ceiling as the full roar of the lynch party beat up the stairway. Kingmead stepped to the center of the room and tilted his head. An ax tore a gaping hole in the plaster; through the turmoil he made out Izee Beulah's labored, hurried words. "One more second, kid. One more hack at this damn stuff—"

The mob seemed to be jammed in the throat of the stairs, seemed to be checked an instant. Kingmead whirled and dragged the bunk to the center of the cell. Outside of the jail was a call for a rope, a woman's scream, and the glow of a lantern. He stood on the bunk barely seeing the jagged aperture in the plaster. Izee was head and shoulders through it, a blurred bulk in the darkness. "All right, lift your arms!"

Izee's fingers brushed him and slid away. A pungent cursing, a tremendous intake of breath. "Once more!" The mob crashed up the stairs. Somebody was already at the door and beating against the iron bars. He stretched his arms and sprang at the same time. Izee's biceps snapped, the loosened plaster fell in bunches, filling Kingmead's nostrils and stinging his eyes. He hooked his elbows against a two-by-four beam and drew himself through the aperture. A ragged edge of lath caught and held him at the hips. Below, Lusk's booming bellow filled the cell and the iron door fell against the floor, torn from its hinges by what sounded like sledges. Izee clawed at his waist, swearing steadily; Kingmead felt his partner's sweat dripping on his neck. Then the clinging lath gave way and the two of them were sprawling across the attic beams while a cold draft of air poured through the hole in the shingles. "Up an' out!" wheezed Izee.

"Hustle!" Kingmead pushed his partner through and followed him. The sky and its clouded stars stretched above them. Guns roared in the cell.

They rested against the steeply pitched roof, holding to the ridge. Rube Mitchell's immense bulk was a flat shadow along the shingles and he seemed to be watching the street like a casual spectator. His unhurried greeting slid through the cool night. "Some better up here. Never did see Sun Ford from a bird's-eye view. Improves it a heap. What's them yahoos so agitated about?"

"Horses out behind the stable—behind the stable's corral," muttered Izee. "The rest o' the boys is waitin'. We better skip."

"Spread," muttered Kingmead. "They know where we are. Hear 'em? Scatter. Everybody a different way. I'll meet you there. Go on—go on!"

Izee inched along the ridge and was lost from sight. But Rube Mitchell tarried. "Got to give you a gun, kid. Brought an extra—"

"I've already been donated one. Break away, Rube."

Rube scorned to crawl. He released his grip on the ridge and slid downward as if propelled from a catapult. Hugh heard the man's body rip across the eaves and then thump against the ground hard enough to break bones—but not Rube Mitchell's bones.

The mob surged through the jail and back down the stairs, every timber in the place shaking with their tread. Bullets ripped through the roof as Kingmead straddled the ridge and hopped to its very end. A four-foot alley made a chasm between him and the flat roof of the adjoining saloon building. Rising, he made the jump and landed asprawl. Across it he raced and came again to an alley, this one too wide to be hurdled. But above the saloon and at the back side was a porch that would let him safely to earth. He took that course, lowering himself by a cornice, swinging past the ledge of a window, and revolving down a porch post. He was on the ground, safe in black shadows.

The mob had split into search parties. He heard men swing through the alley he had jumped across. He heard them strike the litter of barrels and boards not twenty feet away. A lantern's glow veered and guttered in the night, approaching from another angle of the back lots. They were evidently patrolling this side of town thoroughly. In another moment he would be boxed. So he turned and ducked along the far edge of the saloon and came to the street, still sheltered by shadows. The livery stable was four buildings removed and to reach it he had to cross the outflung beams of light from the hotel windows, to go through and past a hundred men along the walk.

He shook the plaster from his coat, looked around him and went forward. A group of men shouldered through the saloon door directly to his rear and came along at a quick step. Kingmead shoved his gun in a coat pocket and kept a leisured pace, calculating that they would pass him before he left the protecting shadows. He heard them mention his name.

". . . ain't no skin off my nose about this Kingmead duck. Why bust into him an' get a perforation?"

"Better keep that to yourself, Bill. If Gesher gets a wind o' such talk yuh shore will get a perforation. Ne'mind, le's bustle 'sif we had a letter to give this Kingmead codger. Personal, I ain't in no mind to be crucified by Ruby."

"Kingmead don't owe me no money," grumbled the dissatisfied puncher. "But—"

They tramped up and abreast of Kingmead. The inside puncher's shoulder grazed him, then they passed ahead. A group of men spilled from the hotel and confronted the three punchers; another group crossed the street and joined in. Staccato phrases followed one upon another; an order crisply spoken split the assemblage into fragments. By twos and fours they spread away, some advancing toward Kingmead, some ducking into the alley beside the saloon. A shot cracked out of the back lots and for a moment it loosed every uneasy trigger in that direction, creating a tremendous racket. Those scattered in the street broke for the rear side of town and left the street almost deserted. Kingmead saw nobody on the hotel porch, nobody near the hotel's lane of lamplight. It would take him two long strides to pass that revealing yellow finger; he tipped his hat lower on his face and walked onward. The light made a plain target of him and in the interval every muscle of his body constricted and his heart beat small and quick. Then he was beyond it and in front of the stable. No light burned here; inside was a deep, opaque pool of shadow. He entered and came to a halt.

Instantly he knew someone stood near. He knew it by a faint suspiration of breath, by the small, sibilant abrasion of a boot on straw. No more than a yard removed from him—hardly beyond arm's reach. The warning was so clear and distinct that he swung his body aside and reached for the gun in his coat pocket. A horse stamped in an adjoining stall; a pair of riders galloped along the street. Another shot beat out of the back end of town and the echo was muffled and lost in the stable's pitch-black vault. A murmured challenge reached him.

"Who's that?"

It was a familiar voice, a tantalizingly familiar one. Kingmead stepped inside before answering. "Somebody, maybe, you've been lookin' for. What's your name?"

"Figgered you'd come here to get a pony," was the

still more subdued answer. "I don't guess we'll name any names. Understand?"

This time Kingmead recognized the voice. It was that of Chiloquin Charley. Kingmead wished fervently for a crack of light by which he might see the man's face. Here, surrounded by the full cry of the pack, one small pace ahead of capture, he could not be sure of anything. What did Chiloquin want? Had the man tried to betray him once? In the light of events it didn't seem likely; the scales were tipped in favor of this former partner.

"Where's the stable roustabout?" he asked.

Chiloquin grunted. "I laid a rope around his carcass and stuffed a blanket down his gullet. He's back in the office. Figgered you'd come here and auger for a pony. He dunno who tied him in a package—I did it by dark. They's a hoss saddled in the end corral. Hop to it—back way out."

"Listen, Chiloquin, what's on your chest?"

"It's my own itch, not yours," muttered Chiloquin, and fell silent. Bodies brushed the stable's side wall, figures moved past the entrance and returned. A match burst against the blackness, a cigarette glowed. "Better we shift," muttered one, and they moved on. Chiloquin's breath came out in a long-checked blast.

"That's close enough," he grumbled. "Say, Hugh, I ain't askin' no favors, I ain't askin' yuh to believe anything about me. Only I know where Lusk's got Elmo Starrett cached."

"Dead?"

"Not yet," was Chiloquin's blunt answer. "But if it meant anything in their favor, they'd slit his throat. I reckon yuh heard Lusk say he'd produce Elmo's body by mornin'. He might do it yet, jus' to excite the county more."

Kingmead maintained a long silence. What was in Chiloquin Charley's mind, what purpose lay in his heart?

"I sure wish I knew what was on your chest, Chiloquin."

"Take it or leave it," muttered Chiloquin. "By God, I'm protectin' myself! What for? That's my affair now. But if things break bad for you, then I got to help foot the bill. Mebbe that don't make sense. It will if they hook yuh again. Take it or leave it. I know where they got Elmo. I got two boys out back that'll be straight witnesses."

"What good," whispered Kingmead, half to himself, "are witnesses?" He wasn't thinking of witnesses at the moment. He was thinking of Elmo Starrett dead and what that meant to Helena.

"Take it or leave it," repeated Chiloquin.

"Come on," decided Kingmead.

"Take the hoss and folla me on back. If it gets too hot, I'll jump aboard. The boys are three-four hundred yards to'rds the road."

"No," said Kingmead. "Leave that horse right in the stall. The old gang's waitin' near by. Hit through the back door and around the corrals."

He heard Chiloquin Charley's teeth click. "Izee?"

"Yeah—and others."

Chiloquin swore bitterly. "It won't work. Those boys won't ride with me."

"I'm boss," grunted Kingmead. A thin suspicion rose in his head, a suspicion he smashed with an effort of will. "Go on like I told you."

They walked down the stable's length, ducked through a crack in the sliding doors at the rear, and crept along a strip of ground beaten hard by a thousand hoofs. The corral bars made a dim skeleton outline in front, a hundred stray sounds disturbed the night. But the searchers seemed to have concentrated on a building at the far end of town. Lusk's booming voice carried over the distance, a great glow of firelight flickered and expanded somewhere beyond the jail. Chiloquin's body merged with the corral bars and his sibilant question, "Now where?" ran along the small night breeze. Kingmead went ahead, skirted the circular corral, and came to the far side. Of a sudden he was confronted by horses and men.

"That you, kid?"

"Yeah, Izee."

"Damn near figgered you was took." Izee's murmur rose sharply. "Who's with yuh?"

"Take it easy, Izee. Chiloquin knows where they've got Elmo cached. I'm bankin' on his word. He and a couple others ride along with us."

Silence. The horses stirred. Rube Mitchell's vast body loomed inward. "Hell," grunted Izee. "Ain't you got no sense?"

Chiloquin broke in. "Listen, Beulah, I'm playin' Kingmead's game tonight. I ain't tryin' to horn in. Let it ride."

"Yeah, well, I ain't proud, but I ain't pokin' my head into no traps, either. Since when did you get religion anyway?"

"Shut up," ordered Kingmead. "This is my funeral. Where's the extra horse? Walk ahead of us, Chiloquin."

Somebody gripped his shoulder. "Old times, Hugh." It was Bill Bixby. He heard Dud Mead's voice and when he found the extra horse and climbed into the saddle, Tammy Rice—the headlong trouble hunter of the former days—was beside him, chuckling. "Ain't had any fun since yuh pulled stakes, Hugh. Sure but this is natcheral."

"Heard you was married, Tammy," whispered Hugh.

"Allus somebody defamin' a gent's character," was Tammy's indignant answer.

"What's this, old home week?" growled Izee. That put a damper to the talk. They rode slowly toward the open country with the outline of Chiloquin Charley to the front. They turned into a dry wash and halted by an isolated lean-to. Chiloquin whistled a short up-and-down tune. A pair of riders converged from the lowering background and challenged.

"All right, boys," said Chiloquin. "It's Kingmead and some friends."

"Kingmead's friends, not yours," broke in Izee. "Who's these jaspers?"

He had his answer direct: "That you, Beulah? Gid Petticord speakin'. Alfred Manary with me. What's up?"

They were unfamiliar names to Kingmead, but not, apparently, to Izee, who urged his horse onward a yard. A match flared and Kingmead had a moment's view of a pair of middle-aged men. The light died and in the darkness Izee announced a reluctant satisfaction. "That's all right. I know you gents. But it gets me how—"

"Let it ride." Chiloquin's warning was crisp. "If your memory runs back eight years, Beulah, you'll recollect I never broke a promise."

Kingmead intervened. "Come on. It won't be night forever."

They waited a moment while Chiloquin disappeared around the side of the lean-to. He came back a-saddle and murmured something about turning due east. The bench lay over that way. Kingmead lagged to the rear, content to let Chiloquin set the pace. They rode briskly across the rolling desert, the hoofs of the horses drumming against the sand, saddle gear jingling into the crisp air. The blurred lights of Sun Ford dimmed and disappeared and the tall outline of the bench bore down upon them. Sage smell rolled along the breeze. Izee Beulah slackened his stride until he was abreast of Kingmead. He bent over, softly prophesying trouble.

"A man can desert one camp for mebbe a good reason. But when he deserts the second the angel Gabriel shorely puts a black mark by his name. I'm meanin' Chiloquin. Trouble smokin' up, Hugh. Mark that."

Kingmead said nothing. They swept on.

Chapter Seven

THE CHASE

SUN FORD, THAT EVENTFUL SUMMER'S NIGHT, was ripped from end to end by Gesher's search parties. Houses that had stood abandoned and desolate many years were rummaged, guards lay along the alleys' ends, and fires were kindled here and there to illumine those stretches across which it was thought the fugitive Kingmead must necessarily pass. Gesher sat in his office and from that dim-lighted sanctum issued his orders to Ruby Lusk, whose fury touched everyone and everything. Lusk refused to believe Kingmead had got free from Sun Ford and in pursuance of this idea he created havoc wherever he went. An ordinary man would immediately have made a dash for the open country. But Lusk had crossed with Kingmead before and he knew that his quarry had a swift and dexterous facility for doing the unexpected.

As the search narrowed down to the south end of town —that end where the stable was—his temper rose to immense heights. Lusk had a certain pride about him, and a certain conceit. He had bullied the county for many years.

He had matched his strength against all who dared oppose him and he had won. Out of this grew a fixed habit never to dignify a quarrel with anger. He laughed at the county; he sported a rough humor, saying in so many words that the man did not live who was formidable enough to arouse his rage. That was his conceit and he knew it was as effective a weapon as his gun.

Yet from the moment of Hugh Kingmead's appearance in the county, Ruby Lusk lost his deliberate poise. In neither of his recent encounters with Kingmead had the man felt ease or assurance. Kingmead had bested him before. Kingmead was his equal, and the knowledge touched the brute instincts in him. His savage desire to crush and utterly destroy was at the same time tainted with fear. Like all gunmen who rose to the top of the heap, Lusk's power was half achievement and half tradition. Men who faced him in a gun fight were handicapped by the legends surrounding him. It weakened their muscles and unsteadied their nerves and Lusk, knowing this well, played up to his part.

It was different with Kingmead; that man refused to be bluffed by legends. Deliberately he was placing himself against Lusk, deliberately inviting an issue. And in his heart, Lusk was not sure he could beat Kingmead to the draw. Therefore he raged about Sun Ford, putting the fear of God in those he commanded. Once Kingmead proved to the county that Lusk was not a superman, there was no telling what the reaction might be. Many of those punchers who rummaged the shadows this night only did so out of necessity. Once the spell of Lusk's power was broken, some of them would turn. Lusk knew it and his words bit into them like a bullwhip's lash.

They came wandering back from all angles of the town, empty-handed. Lusk seized a lantern and headed for the livery stable. "Come on!" he boomed. "Half o' you yellabellies run out-back an' circle the corrals. I sent yuh there before but yo're too damn afeerd o' Kingmead to get offen the main street. Hurry up! Rest come along."

He stopped at the mouth of the stable and lofted his lantern. Others passed him. More lanterns glimmered and dipped through the black vault. "See if any stalls is empty," rumbled Lusk. "Get some pitchforks and jab into the hay. Go on up there, go on! I got a damn good notion to set fire to this trap. He ain't far off, that's a cinch. Neither is the rest o' the bunch which helped him outen the jug."

"Hoss saddled here," murmured a puncher down the line.

"Saddled an' waitin'," grunted Lusk, smacking his lips. "Some rotten double-crosser in this man's village did that! Sift out back. Up in that hay—up in it!"

He turned, walked to the small office in the corner of the stable, and kicked open the door. The lantern cut a broad arc across the shadows and dropped to a table. The roustabout, a weathered and skinny old man, lay on the floor, tied and gagged. A strangled sound came through the gag when he saw Lusk and his faded eyes gleamed queerly against the yellow light. Lusk tilted his head aside and looked down, making no motion to release the roustabout from his bonds. Instead, he laughed, the echo striking harsh and flat against the walls. The roustabout stopped his frantic efforts and was as quiet as one dead. Lusk's bruised features twisted.

"Jemmy, yo're too slick. Yuh don't fool me. How could a hoss be saddled an' waitin' out there unless you did the saddlin'? It don't work. Yuh let 'em tie yuh. Yuh always did buck me, Jemmy. I've been told some o' the statements yuh made. Yo're crooked—crooked as hell. I ain't even goin' to untie yuh. Ain't even goin' to ask no questions."

The roustabout shook his head violently. Lusk grinned and turned to the door, crowded with punchers. "Get out and close that door!"

He waited, his flattened features constricted, chest rising and falling with the turmoil of his passion. Kingmead had bested him again, here was the evidence of it. He was by no means sure this ancient roustabout was in sympathy with the fugitive but he suspected as much, and to Lusk suspicion was the same as proof. He had to smash something, he had to satisfy the burning hunger to hurt somebody, and this roustabout was the nearest victim. There was a quirt hanging on the office wall, a vicious thing with lead pellets beaded through the buckskin throngs. He took it and stepped toward the prone roustabout. The latter made a tremendous effort to free himself—tremendous and futile. And he forced another jangled sound from his throat as the quirt struck him across the face. After that for several moments the little office pulsated to the dead and sickening sound of the quirt striking flesh. And Ruby Lusk's breath rose and fell in great gusts.

Finally Lusk stepped back, throwing the quirt across the roustabout's motionless body. Blood gleamed in the lantern light. Lusk stared at it with a sullen eye and turned and opened the door. Sweat ran down his forehead and the passion of vengeance inflamed his murky eyes. He spat at the waiting punchers, "What in hell yuh idle for? He's in here somewhere. We're a-goin' to burn the damn thing down an' barbecue him."

"No, he ain't either," suggested a puncher reluctantly. "We found tracks out behind the corral. They lead straight toward the bench. That's him and his partners."

Another puncher elbowed through the crowd. "Gesher wants to see yuh," he announced.

Lusk turned out of the stable and rolled down the street to the store, men following silently. Gesher sat as usual in the back room of his place, thin and putty-colored face tipped toward a wall. Lusk, for all his towering anger, waited obediently for the other to speak. Gesher liked to take his time and dictate the conversation.

101

"Well?"

"Gone," muttered Lusk. "His partners got him plumb clear. Toward the bench."

Gesher nodded as if he had expected nothing less. "We will find him and bring him back," he said calmly.

"Why bring him back?" Lusk wanted to know. "We made a bobble doin' that last time. That gent is smoother'n a peeled onion. All we got for our trouble is a jail with a hole drilled in the roof. It's a blamed sight easier to—"

Gesher's glance stopped Lusk. The storekeeper looked sidewise through the door and down the darkened room. There was nobody inside; the punchers were dimly to be seen clustered on the front porch. Lusk moved over and closed the door before taking up his unfinished sentence. "—easier to drop him where we find him."

"I think, perhaps, that would be best," murmured Gesher. "Collect all the men you can, split them into five or six posses, and send them out different ways. Put two or three of our own hands in each posse. You may tell them, on the side, that if they find him they needn't bring him back. On the quiet, understand. No need to have men of the other outfits know that. They're all with us, but it is best to do this discreetly. And now—"

He pursed his lips and touched his finger tips together as if he were praying. Gesher often gave that impression of piousness, a kind of dry and bloodless meekness of spirit. "As to Elmo Starrett—" He paused again.

Lusk watched him closely and in a little while ventured a guess. "He's nothin' but trouble to us, Gesher. Supposin' he gets loose or we should let him go. That story won't set well with the county, will it? We got to go through with what we started."

"That's what I meant," Gesher answered in a sleepy voice.

"Meant what?" Lusk demanded.

Gesher raised his head and the two of them exchanged a prolonged glance. No matter how blunt Ruby Lusk might be, he understood completely the meaning of his boss. He ducked his head in comprehension.

Gesher pursed his lips again and said, "Yes," as if he meant amen. "How many boys you got taking care of Elmo now?"

"Three."

"To be trusted?"

"I picked 'em a-purpose," replied Lusk.

"Ah. Well, go along. Take three or four of the oldest and coolest heads with you. When your chore is finished, get right on Kingmead's trail. He's no fool, Lusk. He may skip the country before we close on him."

For once Lusk openly and bluntly disagreed with his boss. "Don't misguide yourself none with that notion. He's got four-five friends ridin' with him. He's got an idea in his head to bust this neck o' the woods wide apart. Leave? Hell, he ain't got no intentions that way atall. He's on the warpath. I shore wish yuh hadn't been so legal about wantin' him in jail. We had our chance once. It mebbe ain't goin' to be as easy as fallin' off a log next time."

"Go about your business," snapped Gesher, and turned his back to Lusk. "You've got a hundred men to station around this section. I'm not listening to excuses. Understand?"

"Yeah," grumbled Lusk, stumbling down the dark store. He summoned the men of the town to the saloon, detailed posses, and marked out their routes of pursuit. He whispered private instructions to those who were on Gesher's payroll. He sent them away and crooked his finger at the barkeep. And for quite a while he drank his liquor, somberly staring back at himself from the plate-glass mirror behind the bar. Presently he gathered three staunch and chosen members around him, muttered briefly, and led them out. They swung to saddle and galloped deeper into the night, bound toward the bench, and their path was almost directly over the set of tracks made by Kingmead's party, who had passed that way not a half hour previously. A coyote howled dismally; the lone chant quavered along the night wind.

Chapter Eight

THE FIGHT ON THE BENCH

"Hold it."

Chiloquin Charley's warning floated softly back to them; the cavalcade came to a halt. A horse champed on its bit, a boot tapped against a stirrup housing, and these sounds floated upward and outward like ripples across a pond. Chiloquin had moved away, the shadow of man and horse merging into the pooled blackness of the trees. They were high up, twelve full miles from Sun Ford and a thousand feet above the valley floor. They had climbed to the barren bench, threaded its undulating surface, and had now penetrated the pine slopes beyond and above. The air was crisper, the stars were flung across the remote heavens, gleaming like diamond dust yet giving scant light to the world below. Of a sudden they heard the remote sound of water guttering down some stony draw. Izee drew a breath and murmured, "I don't like—" and stopped. Chiloquin Charley drew nearer.

"All right, follow me."

They went on, turning off the path they so far had traveled and down a lesser trail that led them deep into the timber. They dipped and rose with the slopes, they turned and twisted. Somewhere was the hint of firelight—an imperceptible shuttering of the shadows on their right flank. Chiloquin whispered and the column halted, horses colliding. "We walk from here," murmured Chiloquin.

Kingmead dropped to the ground, thinking ahead. There might be a fight over there. They might want their horses in a hurry. Somebody had to stay behind for this purpose. "You two fellows that came with Chiloquin wait here with the brutes. If we raise a shout, come on down."

"Damn a man that makes me walk," grunted Izee. Spurs jingled. Afoot they went like Indians through the timber and to the edge of a creek. Twenty yards along that creek they skirted a bend and stopped. Ahead of them a campfire cut its yellow pattern against the night. A man crouched beside it; other figures lay blanket-wrapped within the circle of light and horses stood just beyond.

The group crept together. "They got Elmo over there," whispered Chiloquin. "Ruby caught the kid yesterday after he tried to pot yuh, Hugh. Brought him here. They got him hogtied. They's three of Gesher's right-hand gunmen chaperonin' him. All right, it's up to you."

"You bet it is," said Izee. "How do we know they's only three Gesher boys in that camp? The shadders may be lousy with 'em."

"I said only three," rejoined Chiloquin, strangely patient.

"Yeah, I heard that. But mebbe more came since yuh saw 'em last." Izee was politely suggesting that Chiloquin was no man to be trusted. The group gathered the hint and thought silently upon it. Rube Mitchell laid his vast frame on the ground and dipped his muzzle in the creek for a long, audible drink. Izee groaned. "Gossakes, Rube, leave some o' that water for the valley folks to irrigate with. Yuh sound like a horse in a trough. Hugh, what's the program?"

"We need Elmo in our business, boys. And those three dryland pirates will make good witnesses. We're goin' to take 'em."

"Idea is fine," acquiesced Izee, "but your expectations ain't normal. Yuh won't get no testimony from them hard-baked fellas."

"Well, we'll enjoy their company anyhow. Now. Rube and Izee—you two circle around the camp to the left. Bill and Dud and Tammy, same to right. Be careful not to go beyond the horses or they'll pick your smell off the breeze. Chiloquin and I'll creep straight on from here, wait five minutes, and bear down on 'em. When you hear me start talkin' to the bunch it's your cue to close in." Then he had an idea. "Chiloquin, maybe this ain't your fight. Stay out of it if that suits you better."

"I got a debt to pay," muttered Chiloquin. "I'm in this jam."

"It shore must be a bad debt," grunted Izee.

Chiloquin met this in silence. Hugh Kingmead, knowing the man's former temper, marveled at Chiloquin's forbearance. He jabbed Izee with a warning finger and his friend snorted and held his peace. Kingmead studied the fire a moment. "All right—sift out. I'll wait five minutes."

Rube Mitchell's practical mind dwelt upon future possibilities. "Supposin' some o' them yahoos don't care none about bein' took? Yuh ain't too particular about demised witnesses, are yuh?"

"If they make a fight of it," decided Hugh, "we'll have to shoot. But it's Gesher and Lusk we're smashin', Rube, not these damn fool riders. So go easy."

"Santa Claus himself," grumbled Izee and moved off.

Hugh listened until the sound of their progress had died. Chiloquin had nothing more to offer and so they waited, watching the fire. The man beside it stirred, rose, and walked casually out of view, beyond the horses. Presently he returned with an armful of wood and poked the flames to fresh activity. Hugh shook his head as he saw the arc of light widen and creep beyond the creek. His partners would not be able to come as close, nor could he manage to approach as near as he wanted. More chance of a fight and somebody being hurt, which he didn't desire. These fellows were only little cogs in Gesher's machine.

"Let's go," he murmured.

They crawled forward on hands and knees for half the distance, then dropped flat. The fire-tender stretched prodigiously and settled down to roll a cigarette. Kingmead had a better view of the men sleeping. Two of them were together, a third was on the opposite side of the blaze. That, Kingmead guessed, would be Elmo Starrett. He thought he saw a rope around the boy's boots but he wasn't sure. By now Izee and the others should be within striking distance.

The horses moved restlessly. Up in the trees there was a clear echo; the fire-tender sprang up and moved back, reaching for his gun. The sleeping ones reared from the blankets. Brush rustled and a call flowed down the slope. Kingmead's muscles tightened. That was Ruby Lusk's voice. A moment later the squat gunman rode into sight with three others behind. They dismounted, their talk reaching out and touching Kingmead. It was a little too far to make out what they said; all Kingmead understood was one word that Lusk flung over the flames: "Starrett." And then Lusk turned to the solitary figure in the blankets and kicked him with a boot's solid blow. The blanket flew aside and Kingmead recognized Elmo—tied hand and foot, features drawn and bloodless.

"That makes seven of 'em," muttered Kingmead. "Which is an equal scrap. The boys'll wonder if they ought to go on or not. If they come back they won't find me. If some come and some stay it's goin' to be too bad. Chiloquin, we're all balled up."

"Lusk's a queer gent," whispered Chiloquin. "Sometimes he won't fight, sometimes he will. He don't like to argue when they's a drop on him—unless he's scared. Then he'll make a bust. He's afraid o' yuh, Hugh. He'll try to make a play."

"You bet he will," said Hugh. He watched the group with a jealous eye, weighing the possibilities. For one odd moment he struggled with a suspicion. What was in Chiloquin's head? Lusk had appeared on the scene almost too promptly; there was an air of doubt about this affair. But, as before, he threw the idea out and considered the camp site carefully. All seven of the men were around the fire; Elmo Starrett lay ten feet away, too discouraged or too tired to speak or move. Kingmead rose to his feet and drew his gun. "Come on, Chiloquin," he whispered.

They stepped through the shadows softly. The time had arrived; Lusk's men were on the verge of splitting and this chance would not come again. Crawling was too slow. On the very edge of the firelight, twenty feet removed from the group, Kingmead came to a halt, and his voice rang across the area like a bell.

"Hands in the air—up in a hustle!"

And, as if the command had struck against a soundingboard, it came smashing back to him from both sides of the fire. "Reach for it, brothers!" That was Izee's challenge, taut and brittle. Bill Bixby's nasal summons crowded hard after: "Yo're boxed, by God!"

The group around Lusk broke as if a bomb had struck. There was not so much as a second's hesitation. The seven men stampeded, each heading for the nearest fringe of the night's shadows. And as they ran, guns gleamed dully, oaths went snarling over the air, and the peace of the hill was battered and shaken by the reverberation of plunging, recklessly aimed shots. Lusk's glistening cheeks turned a complete circle as he sought the outer darkness; his bellowing voice rose above the confusion of the fusillade: "Box who? Knock 'em down! Get Kingmead!"

It was to be a stand-up fight, then. Kingmead swore and sent a bullet after the squat Lusk. Izee and Bill Bixby wavered into sight and as quickly were lost somewhere beyond the horses. Rube Mitchell, the most methodical and cool-headed of them all, called out from beyond the creek. "Number one! I thought these gents had guts!" Kingmead whirled and raced toward the place he last had seen Lusk. There was a tremendous explosion of breath in his face and the outline of an enormous set of shoulders charged him. That was Lusk, galloping like an outraged rhinoceros. Kingmead pulled himself aside and out of the man's path. The flash and roar and powder stench of a bullet struck his senses; then Lusk closed in, cursing in terrific fury. Kingmead's gun flashed up and came down on solid bone. Lusk fell as if shot.

Kingmead dropped to a knee and took possession of the gun that had fallen with Lusk, meanwhile hearing the fight scatter up and down the creek's bank and grow less violent. A moment more, another double burst of shots, and it was over. Rube Mitchell walked into the light with two of Lusk's men ahead of him. Bill Bixby and Tammy returned with two prisoners between them. Dud Mead appeared a little later empty-handed. Izee was missing and so were two of Lusk's crew. Chiloquin had never been more than a few yards from Hugh Kingmead during the short and grim struggle. "Watch Ruby," grunted Hugh, and walked to the fire.

"One of 'em is totally punctured," announced Rube Mitchell. And as a necessary but casual afterthought he added, "I punctured him. Out by the crick."

"Another gent got clear," offered Dud Mead. "He took a couple hacks at me with his gun an' pulled stakes. Me, I follered until I got tired o' runnin'. Last I heard was Izee foggin' on his tail. Izee's a stubborn damn fool."

"Get their horses and tie 'em aboard," directed Kingmead. "Get away from this fire. That missing fellow might circle back and pot somebody." He walked toward the creek. Thirty yards through the darkness he stumbled over a body and knelt down. Rube's shot, he found soon enough, had been fatal for this one of Lusk's crew. The man had died when the bullet hit him. Kingmead returned to the light, somberly sorry. The fellow had been old enough to know which side of the fence he wanted to be on, but it was regrettable he should die for so poor a purpose. His passing didn't change the course of this bitter contest by an inch. He was only an accessory; it was Gesher and Lusk who held the county.

Rube Mitchell, serenely guarding the prisoners while the rest of the partners brought up the near-by horses, saw Kingmead's face. He spat in the fire and issued one of his shrewd comments. "Why take it hard, kid? Yuh can't get a new deal without tearin' up the old deck. It was us or them. Shore as shootin'."

"Yuh damn right," muttered one of the prisoners. He favored Kingmead with a hard and sullen glance. "Yo're Kingmead, huh? First time ever I sot eyes on yuh. I've heard tell yuh was some shucks at scrappin'. Never believed it till now. Well, yuh ain't slow, but don't get no foolish ideas. Us boys is only a drop in the bucket. Gesher'll have your hide out to dry plenty soon."

"Shut up," grunted Rube Mitchell, "'fore I bash yuh. Get aboard them horses an' look pleasant. When I fight I don't like to take prisoners. It's unhandy as hell. Yo're lucky. You fellas ain't got no idee how horrible this war is goin' to be. If yuh think Ruby Lusk is mean jus' wait till yuh see Hugh and us wade into Sun Ford."

"It'll be a cold day," jeered the prisoner.

"I should've cut off your ears," Rube replied with an apparent sad tolerance. "Haul in your neck. We aim to give yuh some lessons in bein' tough. Get on that horse!"

Brush crackled. Izee, hatless, scratched about the face, and with half of his shirt missing, came into sight. He had gone on a long quest and he had returned with game. The missing Lusk partisan ambled in advance, the figure of weariness. Izee looked bruised, but his prisoner was in far worse shape.

"When I got to walk," he observed grimly, "it makes me mad. And no son-of-a-cross-eyed-skunk can lead me a wild-goose chase without gettin' the worst of it."

"Yo're shore a stubborn cuss," said Dud Mead. "I wouldn't run that far to catch a Spanish stallion."

"No, I ain't stubborn," denied Izee. "I'm just set in my ways. Where's Lusk?"

"Still dreamin'," called Chiloquin.

Izee broke one Biblical commandment with a sulphuric torrent of profane and biting adjectives. Kingmead sent a long call through the trees to where the ranchers were stationed with the horses. Then he turned his attention to Elmo Starrett.

The youth had said nothing all during the checking-up process. Tied hand and foot, he lay sprawled on the ground, watching Kingmead with a drawn and queer regard. When Hugh moved near, Elmo's slack lips twitched, but there was no relief or friendliness apparent in his eyes as Kingmead slit the ropes.

"Lusk bring you up here by force, Elmo?" asked Kingmead.

"Yeah."

"What for?"

"You figger that out," muttered Elmo.

Izee came up and frowned down on the lad. "Kid, yo're a plain damn idiot. Grow up. I'm tellin' yuh information. Gesher had yuh marked for a killin'. So don't be so doggone sour about it. And when yuh aim to shoot a man, don't do it from the rimrocks. Go out an' look him in the face. Say, I wouldn't have your conscience for a mint."

Elmo flushed. Rising, he kicked life into his legs and worked his arms stiffly. "I suppose I'm worse off than I was before. What do you aim to do with me, Kingmead?"

"I know what I'd do with yuh," broke in Izee. "I'd tromp on your britches."

Elmo stared at the fire quite a long while, the partners watching him with open contempt. Elmo felt this and he grew still more crimson. This boy's backbone was not very stiff, he had been influenced and cajoled until all the shoddy qualities latent in him had assumed control. Still, there was decent blood in his veins. And, turning squarely to Kingmead, he did a rare and manly thing.

"I shot at you, all right. But it's been drummed in my head for eight years that you killed Dad. I was going to kill you, only I knew I couldn't do it on an even draw. So I took to the rimrock. I don't know who did shoot the old man, but I'll say now I don't think you did, Mr. Kingmead. I'd like to apologize. Whatever you say, goes. If you'd only shake hands with a fellow—"

Kingmead smiled and stretched forth his hand. "Mistakes will happen. It's all right, Elmo. I knew blamed well you'd measure up if you ever got the chance. Just ride along with us into a little piece of trouble. Izee, give him a belt and a gun."

Izee stared at Kingmead in pained surprise. Hugh's grin broadened, which further agitated Izee. The puncher pivoted on his heels, exasperated beyond control. "Santa Claus!" he snorted.

Chiloquin hauled the unconscious Ruby across the lighted space. "Yuh must've hit him a belt," he observed to Hugh. The giant Rube cradled Lusk in his arms and threw him across a saddle as if he were a blanket roll. They lashed him to the horse as they had done with the other prisoners—feet tied beneath the animal's belly, hands bound and anchored to the horn. The partners looked at Hugh as their own ponies were led up by the pair of ranchers.

"Now where—and what for?" grunted Izee. "We got our company, if that's any comfort to yuh. But if we're goin' into the trappin' business we might as well figger on tyin' down the whole male population of these parts. Where to?"

Kingmead smiled. He was in good spirits again. The first collision with Gesher's power had been disastrous; this affair, as well as his escape from jail, heartened him greatly. He had proven Gesher could be balked and he had concrete evidence that he was not Elmo Starrett's murderer. This was an opening wedge. When this end of the county got wind of his exploit, he felt certain some part of the men in it would modify their opinion about him. And there would be others who, hitherto enforced to silence by Gesher's highhanded tactics, would come over to his camp.

He wasn't sure of the next move. He was yet a little too weak in manpower to ride into Sun Ford. Posses swarmed the range and the hills and these he had to account for, either fight them or win them over—or play a dodging game. He didn't quite know which was the best move. Time would tell. When in doubt, let the other fellow lead. One thing was certain. Lusk was his prisoner and would remain so for the rest of the fight.

"We'll ride a ways back," he decided, "and establish headquarters a little bit closer to town. Let's go."

They climbed into the heart of the hills, each partner riding beside a prisoner. To Izee fell the duty of guarding the still unconscious Lusk and keeping him from capsizing in the saddle. It was not a job Izee cared much about and from time to time his pungent speech sputtered into the night like a fuse. Somewhere out on the barren area of the bench Lusk revived. When he discovered what had taken place he acted like a madman. Kingmead let this disturbance go on until he suspected Lusk was trying to betray the party's presence.

"Figure to raise help, Ruby?"

"They's six outfits on your trail, Kingmead!" stormed Lusk. "It ain't in the cards for yuh to get clear! My time's a-comin' and when it does I aim to crack the marrer outen your bones!"

"Glad to know about those posses, Ruby. Now hush. You've lost your marbles but there ain't any use for you to bawl about it."

"By hell—"

Kingmead murmured to Izee. "See what you can do about it."

"Me?" inquired Izee with a honeyed softness. "Well, I tell yuh; I'm a Democrat and I'm a Baptist. I'm meek, I am. I let folks swipe me on both cheeks, I'm so chickenhearted I can't bear to win at poker, and when I eat beefsteak the tears jes' natcherly rise to think o' the pore orphant baby cows. But if this hunk o' poison lets another yelp outen his bazoo, I'm goin' to take out my gun and I'm goin' to drive his teeth so far down he'll have to chew with his feet. Ruby, hush. Yuh annoy me."

Lusk subsided, for he knew Izee Beulah and he recognized the danger signals in that kind of talk. The cavalcade went on silently, turning away from the trail they had followed previously. Kingmead led them along a winding course; they no longer were heading for Sun Ford but away from it, going in the general direction of the Starrett ranch. The wind strengthened. Kingmead's ears, tuned to the undertone of sound that swept around him, caught the echo of a wavering and a drumming in the deep distance. He pulled up, the party sliding to a halt beside him, and for several moments he waited while the echo grew clearer.

"Posse," muttered Chiloquin, "coming this way."

"Swing off," said Kingmead. They went on at a slow

pace, veering down the bench. Voices carried across the space, hoofs struck sharply. The posse raced above them and on toward the pines. Kingmead turned the course again and spoke softly. "Faster." They swept ahead at a reckless pace, always downward. Once they stopped and it seemed to Kingmead the posse was returning. Izee moved uneasily. "I don't like this game o' tag. Why not brace 'em?"

"Not yet," replied Kingmead.

The bench flattened; they came to a trail and followed it at a dead gallop. A fence swooped out of the shadows and ran parallel, a shed came to view and dropped behind. They skirted a windmill, circled a set of corrals, and drew up before a dark ranch-house. The old Kingmead house.

"What next?" Izee demanded.

"Headquarters. Boost these roosters into it. Hurry up, we're makin' close connections. Ruby, how many's in that posse?"

"Plenty," grunted Lusk.

"Fine. We'll have enough for a tea party. Rustle in there, Rube, and light the lamp. On the front-room table. Dud, amble back fifty yards and keep an ear to the ground. Everybody on the jump."

The back door of the ranch-house groaned on its hinges. Rube Mitchell struck his shins against a chair and swore placidly. In a moment lamplight shimmered out. The partners ripped loose the ropes holding the prisoners' feet, pulled them urgently from the saddles, and boosted them inside. Ruby Lusk turned stubborn and for a little while there was a flurry of words between him and Izee. Izee's patience had been sorely tried. "Ruby," said he, dripping politeness, "will yuh kin'ly amble inside?"

"Yuh'll live to regret—"

Izee snorted. He lifted a leg and planted it forcibly against Lusk, sending the latter sprawling. "Now shut your face and do what I tell yuh!"

Kingmead waited until they were all in the livingroom. He closed the back door and ranged through the lower part of the house, eyes marking the points of concealment off this main room. "Take the guests upstairs. All but Ruby. Friend Ruby is going to be the pot of honey that draws the busy bees. Tammy, you stay up there with them. Rest come back."

He opened the front door wide, pulled a table over so that the lamplight went streaming out upon the porch. He drew a chair beside the table and motioned for Lusk to sit down. Lusk's immense shoulder muscles swelled against the ropes that bound his hands, sweat rolled down his black cheeks, and he stared at Kingmead with a rage that flared the higher because of his impotence.

"You'll bust an artery," warned Kingmead. "I told Gesher not to underestimate the damage I could do. I'll repeat that for your benefit. You've had your innings around these parts. It's my turn now. Sit down."

Ruby obeyed, the fury of his temper abating. "It's a lot of useless labor, Hugh," he rumbled. "Yo're havin' a lot o' fun now, but it can't last. We'll bear yuh down. We got the whole weight o' the county against yuh. How long do yuh figger to be on the top o' the heap?"

"You've got the county buffaloed," replied Kingmead amiably. "You and Gesher think everybody's on your side of the fence because they want to be. You ought to know better. There's plenty just waiting a chance to state their right sentiments and I aim to give them the chance. Ever read what some guy said about fooling the people? The same goes for crowdin' 'em. Human nature is some like a piece of rubber. The harder you stretch it, the harder it flies back. You're about through and so is Gesher."

"Yuh can't bust Gesher's machine," jeered Lusk.

"Can't? I've got a little machine of my own on the make, Ruby. It won't be as big as Gesher's but it don't have to be. You boys are on the wrong side and you know it. That won't help any of you to fight better. You're all in a jam and they'll be a lot of you runnin' for the Border by tomorrow night."

"Fool's talk!" yelled Lusk, turbulent again. Kingmead grinned.

Dud Mead ran through the back door. "That posse's comin' this way. Sounds like a whole hell slue of 'em."

"Block something against that back door. All right, boys, hustle down. The party's about to start."

The two middle-aged ranchers, Chiloquin, Elmo Starrett, Izee, Rube, and Bill Bixby came crashing down the stairs. Tammy, left above on guard, sang out plaintively, "Hey, ain't I in on the fun?"

"Not unless she gets warm," said Hugh. "You fellows scatter. Couple in the kitchen with Dud. Rube, go out the front door and hide beside the porch. Rest in that bedroom. Leave the door part open. They'll circle and see the light. Then they'll see Ruby sitting here with his hands folded on his lap. Keep 'em low, Ruby, so they can't make out the rope. I'll be in this closet and I'll have a gun on Ruby. He's going to tell the gang to come in. When they do, that's Rube's signal to block the front door with his frame and the rest of us step on the scene. Got it? No shooting unless we are shot at. Scatter."

They did. Kingmead slid into the closet, leaving the door open just enough to command a view of Ruby Lusk, who was now left alone. The posse galloped past the house and stopped with the scudding of hoofs. "Tell 'em to come in, Ruby," muttered Kingmead. "Just one bad break and you're a subject for burial. I mean that."

Ruby's head drooped a little. He had his back to the lamp and therefore his hands were shadowed. He seemed a tired and reflective figure as he sat in the center of this cluttered room. Kingmead's muscles were rigid; his gun drew a line on Ruby and he watched the man closely for the slightest betraying move. The posse was afoot and coming nearer. From the sound made and the rumble of talk Kingmead judged better than twenty men to be in the party. Ruby looked out of the corner of his eyes to study Kingmead. The latter ducked his chin in a warning, recognizing the full danger of the man in a situation like this. Sweat trickled down the coppery cheeks and a cold recklessness glittered in the muddy eyes. Lusk was whipping himself to a desperate move; his legs crooked beneath him to support him in a wild spring across the room.

"Dead is a long time, Ruby. Tell 'em to come in."

One of the posse hailed the house. "Hello, there."

"Tell 'em," muttered Kingmead. He drew back the hammer of the gun, the echo of it falling faintly across the silence. Ruby flinched.

"Come on in, boys," he rumbled, and relaxed as if he were tired.

Boots tramped across the threshold. Kingmead's free arm rose to throw open the closet door. There was dynamite in these passing moments. If the temper of that crowd happened to be high or if their nerves were on edge—Counting himself, he mustered ten fighters; it was two to one. The posse crowded closer.

"Where's your gang, Ruby? What's the matter with yuh —what's on your hands?"

The speaker's voice veered sharply upward. "Tied, by the great—!"

Kingmead shoved the closet door wide and stepped through, gun dangling in his fist. He swept the assembled men at a rapid glance, trying to divine the strength of their feeling toward him. This interval had to be bridged swiftly. "I was hopin', boys, that you'd come this way. Wanted to talk with you."

"Get that guy!" roared Lusk. "Get him afore—"

"Watch out, Ruby!" snapped Hugh. "You've done your share of the entertainment. Fall back on your haunches." The men of the posse studied him with pure unfriendliness, with a harsh, intent suspicion plastered on their faces. But none of them had made a move toward their guns. They were sure of themselves, certain of their power. The foremost man, tall and roan-haired, shook his head.

"Shore is interestin'," he muttered. "Yuh got a heap o' nerve, Kingmead. Ain't it sunk into your head yet we're after your hide? How'd yuh come to hogtie Ruby?"

"He got too inquisitive," said Hugh and managed a grin. "What might you boys be wantin' me for?"

The leader shrugged his thin shoulders. "Ain't that a foolish question? Yuh ought to know. It's Elmo—" He stopped talking and looked around the room. "Listen, what's goin' on here? Who's with yuh?"

"It's a trap!" growled Ruby. "They're in them rooms!"

"Hell!" snorted the leader. The posse moved restlessly. Kingmead saw elbows drop.

"Take it easy, it ain't much of a trap. If you want to see the rest of my party, that's agreeable to me. Come on out, boys."

All eyes were turned inward and thus none of the posse members saw Rube Mitchell's towering body framed in the doorway. But they shifted with a suggestive slowness when the rest of Kingmead's party came out of the kitchen and the lower bedroom. A mutter of astonishment swept part of the posse when Elmo Starrett appeared and Kingmead made a careful note of those who seemed surprised. Fully half of the seventeen seemed to have believed Elmo actually dead. The others, then, were a part of Gesher's organization and were in on the secret.

"You don't want me, gentlemen," continued Hugh. "Not for killin' Elmo Starrett."

"No?" grunted the spokesman. "Well, we want yuh jus' the same. What yuh been holdin' the kid out of sight for? Yo're too crooked to get away with it."

Kingmead turned to Elmo. "You tell these fellows what happened to you. Some of them don't know."

"What's that mean?" demanded the leader.

Elmo interrupted. "I tried to pot Mr. Kingmead. I'm sure sorry about that. Afterward, Ruby got the drop on me and rushed me up into the hills. I been there ever since, tied like a turkey. That's Gesher's work—tryin' to rig Mr. Kingmead for puttin' me under. Some of you fellows ought to wake up."

"Yeah?" challenged the spokesman. "Well, we're old enough not to believe that sorter sass. If—"

Izee Beulah, leaning against the wall, hitched himself upright. He pointed an accusing finger at the spokesman. "Listen, Pete Gibbs, I know your history clear back to Noah's ark, and it smells. It smells plenty. Yo're a bought dog, that's what yuh are. When Gesher grunts, yuh jump a mile. Same applies to five other punchers in this here room. But"—and Izee's finger stabbed elsewhere—"I see three particular gents which work on my outfit. Will Nabors, what in hell you and Baldy and Squint doin' in this jam?"

"Who, me?" grumbled Will Nabors. "Why, uh, I tell yuh, Izee, we boys figgered this Kingmead gent had done a murder, so we sorter joined the fun."

Izee's words dripped sarcasm. "Honin' to get your nose burned, I guess. Well, if yuh ain't able to tell skunks from house cats I guess I got to act as wet nurse. Now you three waddle to this side o' the room. Kingmead's a white egg. Come on."

"Stop that!" barked the mob's spokesman. "Stay put, you fools."

But the three quite slowly worked away from the main party and aligned themselves against the wall. "I dunno this Kingmead fella," confessed Will Nabors, "but it's plumb plain he didn't shuffle Elmo Starrett off the map. So that's the end o' the party for me, personal. Anyhow, what my ridin' boss says shore goes. On the job, Izee." And the other two mumbled assent.

Ruby Lusk kicked at his chair and rose. "This palaver ends right here. Gibbs, cut this harness offen me."

The spokesman reached into his pocket for a knife, and from the deliberateness of his moves, Kingmead recognized that he was about to bring the issue to a head forthwith. Kingmead stepped toward Lusk. "Get away from there. Ruby stays tied."

"Like hell!"

There had been, meanwhile, a slow cleavage within the mob's ranks. A half-dozen men had drawn away and entered into a whispered parley. Presently one of them crossed the room to the two ranchers Chiloquin had brought along. Kingmead watched them from a corner of his eye. Apparently the two ranchers were well-known characters, even though they had played a silent part all through the evening's fighting and riding. They moved back and joined the six members of the posse. Gibbs, the spokesman, had his knife out, braced defiantly toward Kingmead. And as he started to launch his open defiance, the six possemen openly crossed the room and faced Kingmead.

"Say," said one of them, "it looks as if we've been barkin' up the wrong pole. It's a shore thing you didn't have anything to do with Elmo Starrett. And if he's on your side of the fence, it's plenty plain he don't figger you killed old Colonel Ansel. Which is good evidence for us. We're out of it."

Gibbs swung on them, knife in his hand. "Try that and the county won't be big enough for yuh, see? Get back where yuh belong!"

"Cut this harness!" boomed Lusk. "I'll take care of things. For God's sake, slash it off!"

But Gibbs was not quite sure of himself. The gradual dissolution of his posse had left him, as well as some seven or eight faithfuls, isolated at one end of the room. In the space of five minutes the balance of authority had changed.

Something like nineteen men opposed the handful he could now muster. His sense of security evaporated; he tarried while Ruby Lusk pleaded to be let free.

"Dammit, man, don't let 'em bluff yuh!" cried Ruby. "They's plenty more of our crew upstairs, waitin' to settle this."

"All of which are roped," interposed Hugh Kingmead, grinning. He had, thus far, let the tide roll on. The posse, faced with truth, had disintegrated and given him a clear understanding of his position. "Didn't I tell you, Ruby, that some folks in this county only wanted a chance to break away. Look for yourself. Gibbs, back off. Put up that knife." He turned to the new converts. "You're clear of that gang?"

"Absolutely," said one of the ranchers.

"Want to see this fight through?" persisted Kingmead. "I'm going into Sun Ford."

This produced a further sifting of spirit. Four were willing, but two of them decided they had had enough for one night, electing to go home and be neutral. Kingmead was satisfied. He turned to those of the posse who remained Gesher partisans. Imperceptibly they had given ground and now were bunched near the door, hands swinging at an angle that warned of impending gun play. These were the men who had longest served Gesher. They were the hard characters Gesher had specially chosen for his conquest of this part of the county. And he had chosen well; in this shifting of events, with the odds all against them, they plainly elected to fight it out. Lusk bellowed his encouragement and started to walk toward them. Kingmead's flat challenge checked him. Turning, he saw that he would be between fires. He stopped, dark face glistening in the light.

Gibbs, foremost among the Gesher men, licked his lips. "We're walkin' out, gents. Don't try to stop us."

Kingmead shook his head. "Not that play. Put up your hands and march this way, one at a time. I'm drawin' your stingers. Can't give Gesher any more help tonight."

"We're walkin' out," insisted Gibbs. "That's flat."

Kingmead took a pace ahead. "Why die for Gesher? Forty dollars a month is a poor reason to buy a tombstone. March this way."

Ruby Lusk, still between the factions, flung himself around, crying at his men, "Go at it, boys," and his heavy body smashed against the floor, out of range of fire. An oath exploded and the Gesher men swayed, but above this confusion Rube Mitchell's voice struck them from behind. "Stop that foolishness. Tickle the ozone. I'm awful tired o' roostin' out here."

They had not seen him standing in the shadows of the porch. His challenge broke the tension, diverted their purpose. They were trapped. "March forward, you fellows," repeated Kingmead. "One at a time. This is your night to rest." Defeated, they obeyed.

Rube Mitchell went out to their horses and came back with several ropes. One by one they were tied. Lusk cursed Gibbs fluently, scorched him with bitter accusations of cowardice. Gibbs maintained a stolid silence. Izee Beulah checked them over as if they were so many beeves. "A nice large night," said he, grinning. "You boys ought to be glad yo're out of it. Yuh ain't got no idea how turrible war can be. We're a-goin' to Sun Ford and we're a-goin' to erase that blemish total. What to do with these lads, Hugh?"

"Take 'em along and leave 'em somewhere in town or near town. Can't leave 'em here without a guard of two-three men, which we can't afford now. All except Ruby." He pondered over Ruby's fate at some length. "Trouble is, Ruby, if I take you to Sun Ford and any of your gang see you like this they'll be sore put. They'll fight a lot harder. Some of 'em will. Nobody's got any affection for your tough hide, but they sure will want you free to help 'em scrap. So instead of letting you agitate their sentiments I believe we'll strap you on a bed with about eighty feet of good stout line and let you rest. Fly at it, Izee. Rest of the crowd back on the saddles. Tied."

"With the greatest of pleasure," said Izee. "Upstairs, Ruby. How I hate to do this. My, how I hate it. We'll be back, so don't get lonesome."

Twenty minutes later, Kingmead rode northeast toward Sun Ford. There were seventeen stout and worthy fighters flanking the long row of prisoners. With these men he hoped to demonstrate his power to match Loren Gesher and thus rally the decent element to his standard. He hoped to do it without fighting, for he knew that many of Gesher's paid gunmen, seeing the handwriting on the wall, would flee the country to escape retribution.

But in the general clean-up Kingmead had failed to take one man. This rider, a faithful follower of Lusk, had lagged behind when the rest of the possemen entered the house. And from outside he had heard trouble immediately develop. Being canny and weatherwise, he waited the turn of events. Later he saw Rube Mitchell outlined in the door; he had his chance there for a shot but events had moved too swiftly and he had placed himself too far off. Very cautiously he slid beside a bunkhouse, leading his horse, and there waited. When Kingmead's party swung away with the prisoners, this fellow went inside the house, heard Lusk threshing upstairs, and cut the squat renegade out of his toils. Lusk took the man's gun and horse, thanked him with an oath, and raced in pursuit. A mile onward he branched to another trail, one that would cut around Kingmead and let him into Sun Ford first. It was then well past midnight.

Chapter Nine

THE STRUGGLE FOR SUN FORD

A SOLITARY LIGHT BLINKED OUT OF SUN FORD. The wind had died and the shadows were paling—a sign that this night had reached its climax and would shortly fall into that opaque blackness preceding dawn. Sage smell, held fast in the damp and raw air, rolled against Kingmead's face and filled his chest, the fragrance of it like a stimulant. The land lay locked in a silence and a mystery so deeply felt by riders of the range that in time it became a part of them, flavoring their talk, influencing their acts. It exerted a tremendous power, for it had passed three thousand miles to fill Hugh Kingmead with a hungry homesickness and to trouble his sleep with the familiar images of his former life: the orange spiral of a night fire, the gaunt outline of a juniper, night's dew a-sparkle on the bunch grass. And it had drawn him back; once known and felt, life became barren and tame without it. It stamped the sons of the high desert forever.

A dog in the town barked, echo beating the air in sharp waves. The party approached the dim skeleton of a corral. Kingmead murmured and the riders halted, Izee's muffled question sliding up from the rear. "What now?"

"Changed my mind about our guests," said Kingmead, watching the lone light ahead. Somebody moved across it, cutting off the beam momentarily. Sun Ford was not wholly asleep. "We can't be worried with all that baggage when we ride in. Here's a good corral. Boost 'em inside and tie each sucker to the rails, far enough apart so they won't be able to reach each other. One guard will be enough."

"Is that corral plenty stout?" questioned Elmo.

Izee chuckled. This was work he loved to do. "I've seen five thousand pounds of live critter weight smashin' against its sides. You bet it's strong enough. If they get loose from them rails they deserve a medal. Down, brothers, down."

One of the prisoners coughed. Kingmead threw a brittle warning back. "Stop that. We're bein' white to you boys. Don't make any mistakes."

It took twenty minutes to finish this chore. When it came to assigning a guard, there was a mild altercation. Nobody wanted to be left behind, out of a possible scrap. Kingmead touched the party's pride by shrewdly asking, "You fellows afraid to herd 'em? Somebody might put up a scrap, even so. It's a blamed ticklish situation."

An ominous silence. Kingmead conned the list of men. His partners he wanted with him, as well as Izee's three ranch hands. But there was an elderly cattleman in the group who seemed fitted better for this work than for any that lay ahead. "I'll ask the gentleman with the brown whiskers to stick here. He looks pretty responsible to me."

"Don't worry," murmured that individual, lost in the shadows. "They'll stay tied or they'll get fouled with lead. In case o' trouble, Mr. Kingmead, you'll hear three shots from this direction."

"Fine. Let's go, boys."

The party moved on compactly bunched. Izee, ever a man to look darkly upon the future, came abreast of

Kingmead. "We'd ought to've brought Ruby this far. Somethin' tells me we've sorter left the gate open to a heap of trouble. A heap."

"You'd cut a trouble-makin' steer out of a main herd, wouldn't you?" replied Kingmead, still watching the light from town. It vaguely worried him. "Same applies to Ruby. He's the main fighter in the Gesher bunch. Without him, the rest of the crew is lost; they won't be liable to get desperate. That's why I isolated him. Shucks, he's tied down solid. He'll be there when we get back."

"I ain't sure none about Lusk," grumbled Izee. "No rules apply to that gent. I got the feelin' somethin's goin' to butt us hard from behind before day comes."

Kingmead stopped the procession a scant two hundred yards from the Sun Ford livery stable. One more light wavered at the far end of town. He spoke to the crew very quietly. "We're not riding in to blow this place up, boys. We're aiming to show Gesher and the county that one-man rule is finished. First job is to roust out the judge and attorney Best and show them a life-size view of Elmo. That's the end of that indictment. Then we're going to see the sheriff and have a talk with him. I suppose Gesher owns his breeches too. Doesn't make any difference. We're going to bring those fellows out of the corral and put them in jail to cool awhile. Some we'll just hold for future events. Three-four of them we can charge with kidnaping Elmo. That's to show everybody we've got a whip in the game. Then we head for Gesher. I'm givin' him twenty-four hours to remove his headquarters out of town. That's pretty stiff, but he's got it coming to him. We're out to break his grip, understand?"

Izee groaned. "Oh, slap my wrist, Algy! Listen, Hugh, yuh sound like yo're asleep at the switch. That guy moves like a scorpion—fast and plumb mean. What does he care about Elmo Starrett? They got the same old charge over your head—murderin' Elmo's dad. And they'll try to hook yuh on that."

Chiloquin Charley, who had spoken very little all evening, moved nearer. "Yeah," he muttered in a dry, faraway voice, "they'll try it."

"Let 'em," agreed Hugh. "But they won't be able to pack a jury. I'll have something to say from now on. They tried to convict me twice and it didn't work. It won't now. Nobody knows who killed Colonel Ansel. I guess that's going to be a permanent mystery. But I'm willing to go on trial again to clear the atmosphere."

"Yeah," said Chiloquin, and cleared his throat.

"Santa Claus!" snorted Izee.

"Well, that's the program," said Hugh. "We get these little chores off our chest right away. Then we camp in Sun Ford and watch Gesher's machine fall apart. There's plenty of folks waiting to come out and declare themselves against him. When I tell what I know and Elmo gives them his yarn, there'll be a clean sweep. Let's go."

"Yuh been away eight years," observed Rube Mitchell placidly. "It ain't goin' to be so easy. They'll be a fight. I'm glad of it."

"Yeah," droned Chiloquin.

"Let's go," repeated Hugh.

"My feet hurt," grumbled Izee, ominously. For him that was an unfailing sign of grief and hard times.

The party moved in toward the street end. The near light blinked suddenly out, leaving Sun Ford in complete darkness save for that telltale glimmer over by Gesher's store. Kingmead shook his head, disturbed by some queer inner warning. Eight years in the East had dulled his sense of danger; once he had been much like a wild animal in the ability to react to those intangible hints that passed across a room or came down out of a night such as this. He felt a message in the brooding, still blackness of the street. In the old days he would have instantly acted on the prompting of his instincts. Now, he reasoned. And reason, a treacherous thing in this land, bade him go on. The men around him said nothing at all, but he felt the weight of their suspicion strongly. They were spreading out, coming into the street abreast of each other. Izee was to his immediate left, the stolid and formidable Rube Mitchell to his right. Looking about him he saw the shadow they made, completely filling the street from walk to walk, one line ahead and one behind like a cavalry patrol entering alien territory on a scout.

They arrived in front of the livery stable and the soft shuffling of the ponies' feet and the small jingling of harness and spurs sent echoes spurting ahead of them. The light in Gesher's store died. Izee and Rube Mitchell, as if jerked by a string, sat back in their saddles, arms dropping. This town was not asleep; men were abroad, running along the dust. A figure raced toward the posse, a woman's voice cried a warning:

"Hugh—Hugh—be careful! They're waiting for you! A trap! Ruby Lusk—and Ruby's men in—"

Helena Starrett's voice. And Ruby's raging bellow roaring above it. The party stopped, horses swinging to tight reins. Kingmead dropped to the ground and stepped in front of the girl, pulling her behind him at one sweep of his arm.

Of a sudden lights gushed through a dozen windows and they were dimly outlined, targets to be shot at. Bedlam struck the street—mushrooming purple flashes and the reverberating roar of guns, bullets spat-spatting in the dust. And over all this the continual smash and pound of Ruby Lusk's violent, mad exhortation.

"Into the stable!" shouted Kingmead. "Never mind—never mind swapping lead! Get out of this—into the stable!"

He gathered the girl in his arms and ran for the stable's black mouth. Izee was cursing, but Rube Mitchell laughed like a boy let out of school. They crowded through and out of the fire.

Kingmead shoved the girl away from him. "Get back in the hay, away back out of range, Helena."

"There's fifty of them," she whispered, breathing hard. "They were waiting for you to ride in front of the jail. They're on both sides of the street—in the jail and in the restaurant. I heard them talking below the hotel window. Lusk means to kill you!"

"All right. I guess I've got to see him. Now climb into the hay." He swung around to the men. "I didn't want to fight," he said bitterly. "Damn Gesher, it's his conscience that'll be troubled by dead men. Not mine."

Chiloquin's husky voice came strangely through the darkness. "Yeah, conscience is shore a hard set o' spurs. We'll fight?"

"I reckon we've got to," said Hugh. "There's about fifty of them, according to Helena. If any of you boys want to drop out, now's the time. We've got to call his hand."

"Kingmead," grunted Izee, "I've heard yuh make that pass once before. I don't want to hear it again. Shut up. You've forgot a heap in the last eight years."

"Maybe," muttered Hugh. "All right, hitch up your pants. We've got to clean up this mess—"

An excited and shrill phrase broke in. "Hey, boys. I'm taking a deal, too."

"Who are you?"

"Quiggett, Harold Quiggett. A busted-down newspaperman. Boy, how I pine to express myself. Gimme a gun! Gimme a gun!"

Izee had gone to the stable door. He came back with some ideas on strategy. "They're shootin' a lot o' lead but they ain't movin' this way none. How about splittin' the party—half on one side of town, half on the other."

Kingmead vetoed that instantly. "Stick together, every man. Else we'll be too weak. Helena says they're mostly around the jail and restaurant. We'll tackle the restaurant first. Come on."

He walked toward the stable's back door. Helena Starrett ran out of a stall. "Be careful! Ruby Lusk—I have never heard a man so vile, so stark crazy! He whipped the stable roustabout with a quirt. The poor creature died a little while ago!"

"Another mark chalked up," muttered Kingmead. He slipped through the back door and led his party through a back lane. Lights sprang up from second-story windows, the firing slackened. But Lusk's shouting rose and fell like an intermittent storm signal. Kingmead guided himself by it, over broken boxes and around piles of discarded cans and wire. An unmistakable stench struck his nostrils—the garbage barrels of the restaurant. And the rear door of the place stood wide, inviting him into an unknown situation. Only a moment he tarried, a moment in which he threw aside every scruple and quenched his horror of killing. Until Gesher's power was broken there could be no peace, no security. All the brutality and all the despotism—

"Come on. No use trying to use science. It's just smash along." And he ran through the dark kitchen, flung open a swinging door, and collided with some obscure figure. More than one man was in here, waiting. He was swiftly challenged.

"Who's that?"

"Kingmead!"

"By God!" The four walls threw a thunder against his ears. He struck that challenging figure with his whole weight and drove the barrel of his gun downward. Dishes smashed to the floor, powder smell choked him. His own partisans were calling out names; the flimsy structure shook with the impact of combatants reeling against the boards. He plowed on. The very weight of his party emptied the restaurant of Gesher men. They retreated across the street. More lights ran yellow lanes across the dust. Kingmead galloped directly toward the jail door. Izee and Rube had somehow kept track of his whereabouts, for they were beside him now, one fiery and explosive, the other as silent as a judge. So they fought up to the jail door, again the weight of their attack pushing Gesher men inward. Kingmead was bludgeoned by a fist. It knocked him down and he was kicked by struggling feet, stepped on and rolled over. More explosions beat from wall to wall, men crying out identification, men laboring with their passions and spewing up the sediment of their natures. It was a wild, weird, and impossible thing—this contest. Men were fighting without knowledge or sight of whom they struck. A kind of frenzy carried them on, a frenzy that clouded minds and overbore all caution.

Kingmead fought his way off the floor. He was clear over at a corner, jammed against the jailer's desk. Guns roared along the stairs and a heavy fight seemed to be taking place in the cell from which he had earlier escaped. But the resistance down here had wilted; Gesher partisans had escaped through the back way. A kind of calm settled over the crowd. Kingmead rallied them. "Outside again, boys. They're breaking. Follow this up—follow it up! Come on."

He ran outside and waited a moment. Individual fights were scattered all along the street. He heard them, he saw them in and out of the lamplight. And it puzzled him greatly to feel so many men gathering around him. Izee and Rube Mitchell crossed a patch of light, both battered and torn, both with the zest of battle on their cheeks. Izee was anxiously sounding the shadows. "Hugh, hey, Hugh!"

"Here. What's all this mob?"

"Recruits!" shouted Izee. "We got the chaff sifted from the wheat. What's next?"

"Anybody seen Lusk?"

Somebody in the crowd answered that. "I heard him bellerin' over by Gesher's joint."

"That's our station," said Kingmead. "Come on." He ran ahead of them, jumped to the store's high porch, and struck a closed door. One light glimmered through the window. Men whispered behind that barred portal. Kingmead drew back. "Open up!" he shouted. "You're through."

"Like hell!" growled a voice inside. "Come an' get us."

He jerked aside, bullets ripping the panels. Windows were smashed in by the assaulting party. Kingmead hurled himself against the door and the ancient lock gave way, the hinges ripped loose, and the whole barrier fell, himself sprawling across it. Again he was jammed and shoved by the crowd behind. And again the hand-to-hand fighting, with here and there a gun's report marking the struggle. There could be no prolonged resistance; it was smothered by the gathering momentum of those who had joined Kingmead's banner. Hugh pulled himself around a counter, feeling the effects of the jolting he had taken. And then he saw Gesher's office door open and the lamplight coming through. And he saw Gesher seated at a desk, back turned to all this as if he were sublimely indifferent. He hurdled the counter, a pace in front of the crowd; he reached the office and barred it with his arm. "She's over, boys. I'll settle this."

"No, yuh won't. We're goin' to pluck this rooster."

That wasn't one of his partners speaking. It was someone else flushed with the ease of victory. The voice of the mob was making itself heard; this was the end of Gesher's long reign, the final dissolution of his empire. And, like many another despot, he was living through that memorable scene where those whom he once had fed and paid and bullied were turned against him and demanding his sacrifice. Kingmead retreated from the door and drew his gun. "I'm leading this parade, gentlemen. I started it and I'll finish it in my own style. No lynching."

The light fell over his shoulders and struck their faces as they crowded up to the door. Unfriendly faces, and for the time being that unfriendliness extended to him because he stood in their way. Tomorrow they would be normal. Tonight they were drunk. And one of them challenged his authority bluntly.

"Don't set up no deadline, Kingmead. We got into this fight with yuh and we shore aim to see it through."

He couldn't see any of his partners in the crowd and he wondered where they were. "You'll see it through my way," he repeated. "I don't admire to lead a bunch of lynch lawyers. We've won the argument. The details of bookkeeping I'll look after. You fellows seem to forget it's my fight in the first place."

"Step away—we're comin' through."

The alley entrance to Gesher's office flew open. Kingmead whirled to see his original crew come trooping through, Izee and Rube Mitchell foremost. They caught the significance of Kingmead's drawn gun and ranged beside him. Rube's mild eyes stared down at the crowd and he inquired as to their health softly. "Feelin' pretty well? Yeah. Well, better stay that way. We're handlin' this show. If we need more help, we'll ask. Be calm, brothers, be calm."

All this while Loren Gesher had remained as still as death in the chair, never turning to face the crowd. Nor did he do so now. Kingmead, leaving his partners to control the door, stepped around until he was in front of Gesher. Then, and not before, did the man raise his head. His cheeks were sallow, he seemed tired, he seemed to have emerged from a prayer. But there was no fear discernible, no emotion. He looked at Kingmead in the manner of a man facing some applicant for a job.

"What do you want?" he asked in his usual dry, nasal tones.

"You're through, Loren."

"I believe that's right," admitted Gesher. Kingmead had to admire him for the way in which he brushed aside sentiment and came to the hard truth. "But what do you want?"

"You'll pull stakes tonight, Loren," went on Kingmead. "I'm layin' down the law. Draw a line through the middle of the county. You're free to range the west half. This half you're never to set a foot on. From now on."

"All my properties are here, Kingmead."

"I guess you can manage them from Bend as well as from Sun Ford. As for the store, rent it or sell it. I don't care. You've lost this fight and you'll have to take the short end."

"How about those I.O.U.'s?" asked Gesher in a matter-of-fact way.

"Crooked money," grunted Kingmead. But he turned it over and over in his head. "A debt's a debt, I guess. I'll pay you market price. Your stock's away down. Thirty percent, sent to you at Bend."

"Accept," said Gesher and rose from his chair. He picked up a pencil and carefully thrust it into his pocket; he sorted and tied the papers on his desk. And still there was neither anger nor regret to be seen on the putty-like cheeks of this individual who had ruled so much territory and so many men by the barest nod of his head. He looked around the office, as if recalling the pictures and relics on the walls, and pursed his lips, chin sinking toward his chest. Standing thus between the tall and rawboned partners, he looked strangely small and thin and ineffective. The power of Loren Gesher's name had rested in his silence and in the terribly swift thrusts he made through the agency of Lusk. Bereft of this, he was nothing but a dry and drooping little fellow with a face that could not express emotion and eyes that were tired.

His hat lay on the table. He took it and turned, glancing at the crowd beyond the door. He surveyed them in silence a long, long while—those men he had fed and cowed at the same time. And at last, as he turned from them, he spoke. "I often wondered what kept you from doing this before."

He walked out the back way, Kingmead following, and

crossed to a shed near by. Dawn threatened the eastern rim as he came out of the shed with a saddled horse. He got stiffly into the saddle, a drooping silhouette against the skyline.

"Kingmead," he said, "you will make a good boss. All men need a boss." The stirrups creaked to the changing pressure of his body. "Property rides a man hard. I am riding for Bend but"—and one hand described a circle toward the store and the men inside that store—"I will never reach Bend. I have been tired of this for many years. I bid you good-by." He clucked his tongue; the horse moved away and presently carried Loren Gesher into the shadows—into the mystery and the loneliness and the oblivion of the high desert.

Kingmead heard his name called urgently. Ducking back to the store office, he saw Elmo Starrett elbowing through the crowd. "Chiloquin's in the hotel, Mr. Kingmead. He wants to see you. Better hurry."

Kingmead elbowed through the crowd to the street and walked swiftly along the walk to the hotel, many men following after. Chiloquin Charley was lying on the counter, his sharp, bronzed face settling to a fixed cast. Kingmead called his name, but Chiloquin was looking straight at the ceiling and didn't turn his head. When Kingmead reached the counter and looked down, Chiloquin nodded slightly. "I went after Lusk in the scrap," he murmured. "But Lusk got me."

Hugh shook his head, remembering this man as he had been in the old days. And a lump rose in his throat. "Bad, Chiloquin?"

"Can't feel my hands, can't feel my body," said Chiloquin. "Rest of the boys near me—the fellows I used to ride with?"

"They're here, Chiloquin."

"I'm rememberin' those days," muttered Chiloquin. "Well, I jus' wanted to say so-long to the bunch. Happy days, kid. Listen. A man's conscience shore is a sharp set o' spurs. I got to nursin' a careless iron then. You fellows didn't know it. But Gesher caught me with the goods. And he shore made me pay. I wish yuh'd shake my hand, Hugh. Yuh mebbe won't later."

Kingmead took Chiloquin's limp fist. "You'll be ridin' in better company, Chiloquin," he said gruffly.

"Yeah. Gesher shore made me pay. Yuh didn't kill Colonel Ansel Starrett, Hugh. I want the whole world to know it. Gesher made me kill him. By God, I hate to die crooked!"

Izee stepped forward. "Wait a minute. Chiloquin—"

"He's done," muttered Kingmead. He turned sharply away and walked into the street. Chiloquin once had been a partner. They had shared alike and talked as only men living close together could ever talk. *Eight years is a long time*, he thought. *Men change. Nobody stands still. Well, Chiloquin, I'm makin' some allowance. And I reckon Gabriel might. We'll all be ridin' together by-an-by.*

"Hey, Mr. Kingmead."

Somebody came up at an awkward run. In the pale blue light he saw Elmo Starrett's white cheeks. "Say, Mr. Kingmead, you're stayin' in the country, ain't you?"

"From now on," said Hugh gravely.

"Well, take care of Sis. And when you see her, give her my love."

Kingmead questioned him sharply. "Where are you going?"

There was a trace of sullen defiance in the boy's answer. "I made a damned fool of myself in this country. It's too hard living it down. I'm drifting to another range. When I get squared around—four or five years—I'll come back. Say, you'll take care of her, won't you? Nobody could do it better."

"Wait a minute," interrupted Hugh. "Don't be rash—"

But Elmo had turned and was ten feet distant. "No," he called back, "I've played a sucker plenty long. You take care of her."

Kingmead walked on toward the livery stable, perplexed and troubled of mind. Gesher's power was broken, Gesher's men were whipped. Three-quarters of them would slip away and never return while the rest would be good citizens for fear of outraged public opinion. Men had died. It took tragedy to sweep a country clean. Yet Ruby Lusk had escaped. And Ruby was the one who deserved to die. He shook his head. *I guess I ought to be sending out posses for him, but I've got no heart to fight any more. What did I ever leave the range for? It's spoiled me.*

Dawn streaked the eastern hills, sending thin violet rays into the town. A fresh wind swept the raw and pungent air in from the desert to cleanse Sun Ford. He came abreast the stable door and faced it. "Helena."

He was tired to the bone. But the following instant a shock ran through him, a chill swept up his body. A voice came out of the stable's dark mouth, but it was not Helena Starrett's.

"Well, Hugh. Thought I'd run, huh? Hell, I ain't doin' no runnin' till I tip you over."

"Ruby!"

"Same. Now stand there and sweat awhile."

He was trapped, he dared not move. Here in the street he was visible to Lusk. But Lusk stood somewhere within the black vault of the stable, his squat and ugly body completely cloaked. Kingmead leaned forward, trying to penetrate the pall that lay between them. Lusk's grim chuckle came rolling out.

"How do yuh like it, Hugh? How do yuh like bein' crucified? I reckon yuh raised hell with this country, didn't yuh? Busted us wide open. Yeah. Well, kid, yo're goin' to get a reformer's grave. Helena will put some flowers on your box and cry for a good man that's dead. And I'll hunt a new pasture. Always fresh grass over the hill, Hugh. Why didn't yuh leave us alone?"

Sweat stung Kingmead's forehead like needles. His taut muscles ached. Ruby had him cold. Ruby played with him, that grim chuckle rising and falling in the darkness. "Not very sure of your draw, Ruby?" he drawled, the words sounding flat in the damp air.

"Why should I be foolish? How do yuh like bein' crucified? When I'm ready, I'll tell yuh to draw. Try your luck, kid. It's been a long time I waited for this chance. Now that yo're about done I don't mind sayin' yuh worried me all the time. Yo're a good man. Why don't yuh raise your arms, Hugh? I ain't shootin' for a minute or so."

Kingmead marked the sound of the man's speech with a desperate intensity. Lusk was just beyond the door, about the middle of it. He had ten wide feet to guess at and only one bullet to spend on that guess. And Ruby was in there, enjoying all this. One shot wasn't enough. He needed more to explore the darkness. If Ruby—

"Ruby, don't it occur to you there's men standin' in the back way listenin'—?"

He had no evidence that Ruby was turning. It was an old trick. And still the man, secure in the shadows, might actually look around. Kingmead threw his body aside, drawing. The shots woke the morning's lull, beating down the street on the wings of the heavy air. He never counted the shots he threw into that stable's maw, sweeping the square opening, running inward as he fired. Men were racing down the dusty street, calling questions. Guns were touched off elsewhere. Yet of this Kingmead knew very little, for his whole mind was thrown ahead of him and his ears were straining for Ruby's return shot. He heard one sound; then the stable filled and a lantern pitched up and down and glimmered on a sprawled body that looked monstrously out of shape. And blood glistened along a copper-colored face.

"Lusk!"

Kingmead dropped his gun in the dirt and went out, turning his head from the sight of the dead Ruby. The world was a gamble. Ruby had been so sure of life and he, Kingmead, had said good-by to the violet light of this dawning morning. But the world was a gamble and his raking shots had caught Lusk. His boot heel caught on a loose board and he staggered like a drunken man. He was that tired. Helena hadn't answered him; therefore she must be in the hotel, waiting to know what had happened to him, to her brother, and to her future.

A man came crying down the walk behind him. "Gangway, elbow room! Let a broken-down newspaperman get to his copy paper. Oh, by golly—"

Kingmead stopped and threw out an arm as Quiggett went by. "Wait a minute," he called. "Where are you going?"

Quiggett halted and poured words out hotly. "Mr. Kingmead, I've lived in this infernal country twelve months. I've seen good stories and I've heard 'em and never yet have I been able to write one for fear of stepping on somebody's toes and getting soaked in the neck. Now I've got the best story ever originated in this state. Saw it with my own eyes! And maybe you don't think I ain't going to smear it all over my paper and distribute it to the bounden universe. Oh, peaches, here comes cream." He started away.

"Wait a minute," snapped Kingmead. "What are you going to do? Advertise a family quarrel to the whole country and bring a lot of tinhorn investigators down here? That's what your story will do. And folks will think we're a bunch of bad men living on alkali water. It won't do, Quiggett. Don't you touch this affair. We want Gesher's friends and gunmen to sift out of the picture quietly. But if you rub it in they're apt to get their pride up and come back snipe shooting."

He was, for the moment, thoroughly aroused. Tremendous weariness came hard after and sat on his shoulders like leaden weights. Quiggett said something he couldn't understand and he was too tired to ask what it was. He turned into the hotel and called over to the clerk.

"Helena Starrett in, Bob?"

"Number Twelve, Mr. Kingmead."

"I'm obliged." Kingmead plodded up the stairs and down the carpeted hall. He couldn't see the numbers but there was an open door at the end of the hall and a woman's figure outlined against the light. He walked up to her, leaned against the casing. She put out a hand to him and turned in. He saw her face clearly then; he saw a glow in her eyes that seemed to soothe him and take the weights from his shoulders. Her hand brushed his coat, her slow, quiet words were like a cooling, comforting balm.

"Hugh—Hugh. Thank God."

Harold Quiggett, editor and publisher of the *Sun Ford Roundup,* sat before his desk and turned out the following copy for the forthcoming weekly edition of his paper:

Loren A. Gesher, well-known resident of Sun Ford and owner of several surrounding ranches, left town yesterday. Ill health was said to be the cause of his departure. The removal of so old a pioneer will be a cause for regret by his friends.

And also:

Hugh Kingmead, who has spent eight years in the East, returned to his native heath this week. Hugh's arrival was entirely unexpected, but he received a rousing reception that must surely linger in his memory forever. Dame Rumor whispers something to the effect that Hugh may have some sort of future interest in the Starrett ranch. What that interest is may be best left to future judgment. Good luck, Hugh. She's a splendid girl.

Quiggett read the items over; he rose and threw his hat to the floor. He then proceeded to smash it with his feet, saying with an expression bordering on feverishness, "The power of the press. Ha-ha-ha!"